In Jesus' Own Words:
The Sermon on the Mount

Cover design by Stacy Lee
http://www.StacyLeeArt.com

TIM MILLER

IN JESUS' OWN WORDS: THE SERMON ON THE MOUNT

2007

In Jesus' Own Words:
The Sermon on the Mount

TABLE OF CONTENTS

ACKNOWLEDGMENTS

Without the following people, this book would not have been possible. My good friend, Susan Stafford who has been an inspiration throughout the process. Stacy Lee, a talented artist whose spiritual maturity is far beyond her years. Dr. Steve Schweitzer Ph.D for showing me how scripture can come to life, and to Dr. Duane Beals Ph.D for teaching me how to present the Bible to others. Ultimately, I owe everything to our Lord and Saviour, Jesus Christ.

This book is dedicated to my beautiful wife Jami, who continually challenges me to be more like Christ.

FOREWORD

It was in the year of 2001 when I first met Tim. At that time, he was an author of mystery novels. I, too, was an aspiring author, and we often bounced marketing ideas off of each other in a marketing group. I think our only goal in life at that point was to hit it big with our books.

Tim's novels, however, consisted of vulgar wording and murder to describe a perpetrator, and the power of a dominating man was often depicted as the power he could have over a woman. But, in spite of the standing hairs on my spine, I still found that I was unable to put his novels or any of his stories down; they always kept me intrigued.

Somewhere in the midst of that time, Tim contacted me, informing me that he had torn and thrown away all of his mystery novels and had even canceled a current pending contract with a publisher! When I asked him why, he said, "Because I gave my life to Christ. Once I did that, I wanted nothing to do with the old me."

I was somewhat disappointed, because I always knew that his books had the potential to be bestsellers. But then, how could I be sad? He had done something far better. He had become a bestseller with God, and the best part is that his name made something far better than the New York Times list—it made it into The Book of Life!

The ironic thing was that I, too, had at that time transformed and given my life to Christ. We both experienced different circumstances that led us to that point, but we had both come full circle to the center to reflect on what life and love were truly about.

As the next six years in time unfolded, Tim committed his time, efforts, and life to Christ by being completely transformed in mind, body, and spirit. He has demonstrated a true Christlike spirit by writing blogs and developing a web page on Myspace, all in an effort to lead the lost to Christ. He has made himself available to the lost by offering them counsel while working overtime at his job and keeping up with the demands of family and ministry. He has also been taking college courses in Biblical studies.

Friends and readers, I am proud to present this newly refined workmanship of Tim Miller. I have watched him journey from the back list author I met in 2001, who was trying to make it big, to the matured Christian whose only goal now is to bring others with him to heaven. When I see the transformation God has made is Tim's life, it brings tears to my eyes. All I can say is, "Wow."

Susan Stafford
Another Chance Ministries of Susan Stafford
Author, Founder, and President

INTRODUCTION

I thought I would start by explaining how and why I wrote this book. I know there is no shortage of Sermon on the Mount books and Bible studies out there. I don't expect to blaze any new territory. Something that I've noticed in my studies is that many of these works are somewhat academic in nature. There are many good studies out there. However, I felt it would be beneficial to interpret this sermon to the best of my abilities, through much prayer and meditation, and then to share my findings.

I didn't start out with the idea of writing a book on this subject. In October of 2006, I began I Am The Way Ministries. It's a simple prayer ministry on MySpace that can be found at http://www.iamthewayministries.com. My ministry goal is to provide prayer, support, and encouragement to anyone and everyone who needs it. I don't discriminate against anyone who asks me for prayer, no matter how "out there" they might seem.

I also have a blog on the website. There, I began posting some thoughts and Bible studies. I happen to currently be studying Bible and Ministry at Bethel College in Mishawaka, IN. Shortly after forming this ministry, I took my homiletics class at Bethel. For those who are not familiar with it, homiletics is basically the art of preaching (including sermon writing). Well, I was pretty good at it. Before I was a Christian, I used to do a lot of writing, mostly fiction. I had even published some secular suspense novels. However, I had not yet found a way to use my gift until I took this class.

In the class, I found that I was much better at writing the sermons than actually delivering them. I wasn't horrible at the delivery; I just wasn't great at it. So as I wrote my sermons, I posted them on my blog and received a great response from believers and non-believers alike. I offended my share of people, but I suppose that's inevitable.

So, as I was working on my blog, a ministry I attend, called Voice Ministries, delivered a teaching one night on the Sermon on the Mount. I realized at that time that even though I had grown up in church and have attended church regularly for the last three years, I had never actually heard anyone preach on the subject. Why was that? Why would churches and pastors not spend more time on what are Jesus' most well known and probably most important teachings?

When I was growing up, I had Sunday school teachers who sort of dismissed the Sermon on the Mount. "He was speaking symbolically there," or "That just isn't relevant for us today." After really digging into the scriptures and spending time in prayer before each section, I learned quite the opposite. Everything he says in that sermon is quite relevant. His words are more than nuggets of wisdom. They are a treasure chest of knowledge. We would be foolish to ignore them.

My goal is not to produce a heavy, academic exegesis. My intention is to create a simple understanding of Jesus' words. I want this book to be something any person can read and put to use and apply to their everyday lives. So as we begin, I ask that you take the time to pray and ask God to reveal his words to you. Feel free to take out your Bibles and follow along. I pray that this book is a blessing to all of you.

PART 1
The Beatitudes

^{Mt 5:3} *Blessed are the poor in spirit, for theirs is the kingdom of heaven.*

1.

Blessed Are the Poor in Spirit

Are you poor in spirit? It seems as if many modern Christians today have this attitude that God will only bless those who are perfect or who have it all together. If you're struggling, broken, or troubled, then how can you be worthy of God's blessings? In Matthew 5:3, Jesus begins his famous Sermon on the Mount with the Beatitudes. In the Beatitudes, he lists those who are blessed by God, beginning with the poor in spirit. Just what does it mean to be poor in spirit? Is it something we should strive for?

Spiritually poor, physically poor

One thing to note right away is that during Jesus' time, poverty of any kind was not something to be desired. As a matter of fact, it was quite frowned upon. They didn't have the social welfare programs we have today. If you were poor, then it was because you were cursed by God for some reason, and no one would touch you with a ten foot pole. The Pharisees and high priests were often wealthy and dressed in the finest robes. Wealth was considered a visible sign of God's blessings.

Was Jesus talking about simply being financially poor? He was not. He never commands us to become poor intentionally in order to maintain some higher level of spirituality. Matthew 19 tells the story of the rich young ruler. Jesus tells him to sell all his things, give the money to the poor, and follow him. Many take that as a command to sell all our things and do just that.

However, Jesus knew that for this young man, his money was his god. Jesus doesn't tell us we must have no money. He just doesn't want us to seek *only* money either. Seeking God might be easier for the poor, however, because they have to rely more heavily on God's provision.

The poor in spirit realize their need for a savior

Spiritual poverty, then, is realizing that we do not possess the means to save ourselves. Spiritual poverty is recognizing and even being remorseful over our own sinfulness. This is evidenced by Jesus' story of the publican who, in Luke 18:13, fell to his knees and asked for God's mercy. Then you have Gideon in Judges 6:15. He told God he was the least in his tribe. The attitudes of both these men were spiritually humble. They were poor in spirit. The spiritually poor are acutely aware of their need for grace and will look to God for spiritual fulfillment and forgiveness.

So what is the Kingdom of Heaven they will inherit?

Jesus makes many references to the Kingdom of Heaven in his teachings. For most Christians, this is interpreted as referring to heaven and the afterlife itself, which is partly correct. However, this interpretation omits some important things. Today, many Americans don't seem too anxious to go to be with Jesus. We have pretty comfortable lives, nice homes, satellite dishes, and other toys. I remember hearing a person once say, "I don't want Jesus to come back yet; I'm going on a cruise this summer!"

So is the Kingdom of Heaven just the afterlife? I don't think so. When Jesus says, "The Kingdom of Heaven is at hand," he means right now. In this sermon, Jesus was telling us what heaven on earth should be like. We don't have to wait until we die to feel the love and joy of heaven. We can experience that now by being the kind of people Jesus told us to be.

When we become spiritually poor, we are ready to enter the Kingdom of Heaven here on earth, also known as the body of Christ. Just look at what Jesus did with his physical body. He healed, loved, taught, and shared. What are we to do as his followers? It would make sense that we are also to heal, love, teach, and share. These actions foreshadow of the eternal Kingdom of Heaven.

Spiritual poverty is the first step toward repentance and salvation. Once we've achieved this, then we will be open to receiving the other blessings of the Beatitudes. Spiritual poverty is all part of our journey as we take up our cross to follow Jesus. Many teach that salvation is the finishing point. You say a prayer, accept Jesus, and that's it; time to sit back and cruise into heaven. However, in the Sermon on the Mount, Jesus is calling us into action, not lethargy. He is challenging the religious and self-righteous to do more than just appear holy. Spiritual poverty is his first challenge.

^{Mt 5:4} *Blessed are those who mourn, for they will be comforted.*

2.

Blessed Are Those Who Mourn

This seems to be another strange saying. Jesus already blessed the poor in spirit. That alone confused everyone around him. First he blesses the poor, and now he blesses people who mourn? Who wants to mourn, and why is mourning blessed? If you're mourning, then that must mean some tragedy has struck. That's not something most of us want to deal with. I don't think Jesus is saying we should seek out personal tragedies. However, if tragedy does find you, Jesus promises there will be comfort.

Mourning is not just being sad

Movies can make us sad. I remember watching my ill-fated Chicago Cubs fall apart in the eighth inning of the 2003 playoffs. That was more than sad; that was just plain depressing. However, I can't honestly say that I was mourning. Mourning occurs in the face of a major loss or tragedy. When we lose a loved one, we go into a state of mourning. Unlike sadness, mourning often affects our entire body. Sometimes we can't eat or sleep for days. Other people want to do nothing but eat and sleep.

Years ago when a friend of mine was killed in a car accident, I couldn't watch TV or read anything for at least two weeks. All I did was work during that time. I dreaded any form of down time. All efforts to distract or entertain myself were useless. I've always been a huge reader, but during this time, my reading turned into staring off into space for hours at a time. This was how I handled mourning.

Why must we mourn?

I could go on and on here about how we live in a fallen world and how, because of sin, we now have death and suffering. However, I won't do that. Most of you have probably heard that many times before. Most people I know who are actually going through such a thing don't want to hear that anyway. All the talk of fallen worlds and sin doesn't mean a whole lot when you have lost that one person in your life who means more than anything. Knowing this, I will spare you all that.

When we suffer death, loss, and tragedy, those serve as harsh reminders of how lost, fallen and temporary life here on earth is. For those of us who have a relationship with Christ, we know this place is only temporary. When we go through mourning, we know there is light at the end of the tunnel. We know no matter how much we might miss our loved ones, there is still some comfort in knowing we will see them again. If anyone reading this does not know Christ, there is always time. As long as there is breath in the lungs, there is always hope, and you can never be out of his reach. There always is light at the end.

Mourners will be comforted

Once again, Jesus doesn't seem to be referring only to the afterlife. Yes, I'm sure he is saying that when we get to heaven, those who lived lives of suffering, tragedy and mourning will be given extra comfort. But this is not all he is saying. He also seems to be saying that here on earth, God will send us people to comfort us as we mourn. He will also send us to comfort those who are in mourning. Sometimes, he might comfort us himself, but he does also use our brothers and sisters to show each other love. The Apostle Paul tells us:

2Co 1:3 Praise be to the God and Father of our Lord Jesus Christ, the Father of compassion and the God of all comfort,
2Co 1:4 who comforts us in all our troubles, so that we can comfort those in any trouble with the comfort we ourselves have received from God.

God gives comfort to those who need it, to those who mourn.

Mt 5:5 *Blessed are the meek, for they will inherit the earth.*

3.
Blessed Are the Meek

In Matthew 5:5, Jesus blesses the meek. This is a verse that has had many different interpretations. What does it mean to be meek? This word is often misunderstood. Seriously, what do most of us think of when we think of meekness? Do you think of a pro football player, diving in for that game-winning score? Or do you think of some tiny little man with thick glasses who is scared of his own shadow? In this chapter, we will take a look at this verse and see if we can understand just what it is to be meek, what Jesus was saying about meekness, and what this verse means for us today.

What is "meek"?

Often meekness is associated with weakness. People view the meek as doormats, or as people who are afraid to stand up for themselves. The Bible tells us this is not true, however. The word "meek" is taken from the Greek word *praus,* which often means "humble" when used in this context. The problem is, some English translations use the word "gentle" instead of meek. Others use the word "humble." This problem arises because some Greek words are not easily translated into English, so the translator has to rely on context. So let's look at this verse about a humble man:

Nu 12:3 (Now Moses was a very humble man, more humble than anyone else on the face of the earth.)

Now, I'm sure that most of us would agree that Moses was not a weakling. Granted, he did whine just a bit when God called him into his ministry, but most of us do the same thing. Moses started out as what we might consider to be weak, but then he grew in strength, but he still remained meek. As far as gentleness is concerned, here is a verse to consider:

1Ki 19:12 After the earthquake came a fire, but the LORD was not in the fire. And after the fire came a gentle whisper.

The Lord could have announced his presence with thunder and massive force. Instead, he chose a gentle whisper. Perhaps he was setting an example for how we should be. We tend to always be so loud. We are constantly surrounded by noise. God speaks in whispers so that we will stop and listen.

Gentleness and humility are both good qualities. Neither one of them means "weak." When I think of these things, I think of controlled strength. The sort of strength they teach in martial arts. I took tae kwon do as a teenager. Sure, you learn how to break boards and kick things and all that fun stuff, but you also learn how to control force. These lessons served me well at one point in my life.

I was a bigger kid in my teens, so I didn't get picked on by one bully. I was picked on by large groups of smaller kids. I was pretty easy going, so maybe I seemed like a "soft" target. One day after shop class, a group of about four of five of them came up and were knocking my books out of my hands and started pushing me around. This had happened many times before, but by this point, I had been in my tae kwon do class for several months.

So on this day, these kids were picking on me again, and I tried to walk away. One of them put his hand on my chest and said something like, "Where the *@%! do you think you're going?" He pushed me back. At that point, I jumped forward and snapped a standing side kick and stopped my foot just short of the boy's face. Several months before, I wasn't that flexible, but doing that kick was something I had been working on. I was bigger and stronger than this kid, and I could have knocked his head off had I chose to. However, I didn't wish to hurt anyone. I just wanted to be left alone.

So there I stood for what felt like an eternity holding my foot in front of this kid's face. His eyes had this bizarre look, as if he didn't know what to do. I could see the shock on his friends' faces as well. I finally lowered my foot while he said to me, "Dude, we're just messin' around. You don't gotta freak out on us." And they all left. That was the last time they picked on me. I didn't realize it at the time, but I now know I was exhibiting meekness at that moment.

The meek shall inherit the earth

I find this statement ironic because people who are humble and gentle are already content with what they have. Yet, because of their contentment, they will inherit the earth. So many of us are so hungry for things and in such a hurry to get what is "ours" that we often miss the finer things in life. We miss out on time with our families, time with our friends, or just enjoying God's creation. All these things already belong to the meek, and they take the time to enjoy them.

There are so many others out there, however, who, though they may have gained all the finer things in life, are miserable because of what it takes to hold on to those things. We may think that co-worker who isn't trampling over others is a weakling. We might think that guy who drives a beat-up car to work is pathetic. We might be able to learn some things from those people.

There is a lot more I could say about this verse, but I think I will conclude this chapter here. My goal is to paint a picture of what it is to be meek and to clarify common misconceptions. Meekness is not weakness. On the contrary, meekness is one of the tougher forms of strength to possess. We need look no further than Jesus' own life to see a perfect example of this.

Mt 5:6 *Blessed are those who hunger and thirst for righteousness, for they will be filled.*

4.

Blessed Are Those Who Hunger and Thirst for Righteousness

In this fourth Beatitude, Jesus turns a bit of a corner. The first three Beatitudes were about self. Jesus explained how people must empty themselves before God can fill them with his blessings. He told us what kind of people we should become. In Matthew 5:6, Jesus takes the next step: he calls us to action. While so many of us hunger and thirst for things of this world, Jesus tells us to hunger and thirst for the things of God, such as righteousness. It is believed Jesus was basing this blessing on Isaiah 51:1a:

Isa 51:1 *"Listen to me, you who pursue righteousness and who seek the LORD:*

These are the same people Jesus was blessing, those who would seek him.

Appetite for God

Jesus is telling us here how important it to change our focus from the things of this life. We so often seek the things of this world. The media tells us this is what we should be going after. Some of us might seek approval of others, financial success, fame, and fortune. Jesus says we instead should be starving for righteousness, or what I like to think of as Christlikeness.

While we many not be perfect, nor will we ever be, that doesn't mean we can't strive to be like Jesus. Through him, we can do all things. As long as our eyes are fixed on him, even though we may stumble, we are made righteous through his mercy. What is it you have an appetite for? I know that I, personally, hunger for things like sports, TV, and the internet. I tend to spend too much time doing these things and thereby neglecting my time with God. Sometimes I get too caught up in work to thirst for righteousness. These are things God is challenging me with.

Being filled by God

Once we have completely emptied ourselves as directed in the first three verses of this passage, we can begin to hunger for God. Sometimes all it takes is stripping away many of our daily distractions and seeking him through his Word. Once we have turned our hunger toward God, he can fill us with his blessings. When we spend time reading scripture, praying, meditating on his Word, or just seeking intimacy with him, we are opening ourselves to him. In an earlier passage, Jesus told Satan:

Mt 4:4 Jesus answered, "It is written: 'Man does not live on bread alone, but on every word that comes from the mouth of God."

God will fill us with his truth. We might eat a meal, but how long does that last? You eat breakfast, and a few hours later, you are hungry again. Then a few hours after lunch, we want dinner. But God's word says:

Mt 24:35 *Heaven and earth will pass away, but my words will never pass away.*

God's word is eternal. Once we hunger for him and his word, we will never be hungry again. The things of this earth will always let us down. They will always leave us feeling empty and unsatisfied. No matter how much money we have or how famous we are, it will never be enough. God's love and righteousness are always with us and always will be.

Mt 5:7 Blessed are the merciful, for they will be shown mercy.

5.

Blessed Are the Merciful

Here Jesus gives his next blessing to the merciful. While this verse may seem self-explanatory on the surface, it still needs to be addressed. We live in a world of constant tragedy and suffering. All the while, most of us, both Christians and non-Christians alike, seem indifferent to what is happening around us. How many times have we passed a person on the street who may have been hungry or hurting? Sure, many beggars we see on the street may just be out for money and not really as bad off as they seem. But how much does it cost to stop and talk to them for five minutes?

Maybe we know someone at work who is going through a divorce or a difficult family situation. Maybe someone at our church is having health problems. Many times, we don't even bother to visit these people, or to call them and see how they are. A simple act like calling just might make their day.

The heart of man

We are a busy people. We fill our schedules with so many things, yet often we don't make time for others. In our society today, we often view people as either stepping stones or road blocks. We will then decide how we will use them based on how well they fit into our plans. If they don't suit our needs, then we just might push them aside altogether. This is the heart of man. We humans are out for ourselves. We have our own needs, wants, goals, and projects in mind, and we won't let anyone stand in our way. This is our nature.

The heart of God

Jesus by his life is the very definition of mercy. How many times did Jesus stop what he was doing in order to help someone in need? How many times did he take the time to heal a sick or crippled person? Many times, he just stopped to listen to what someone had to say to him, regardless of their status in society. This is mercy in action. Jesus didn't assume anyone who came to him was a freeloader or that he had ulterior motives. He didn't say, "Hey, sorry, but I've got to get to the mount to preach my sermon. I don't have time to talk to you." No, he always took the time and helped whoever he could when he could. No one was too lost for him to love or too low for him to serve.

Blessed are the merciful

So when Jesus says, "Blessed are the merciful, for they will be shown mercy," he's telling us that if we would like to receive mercy, then we should be willing to show mercy to others. What if someone wrongs you, but then asks forgiveness later? Even in the most extreme case, do you hold his wrong over his heads, or do you show him mercy? If we deny mercy to those who sin against us, should God still show mercy to us? The truth seems so simple, yet so many of us have a hard time with this.

In the everyday sense, this means we should go visit those who are sick. We should listen to a person who is hurting. Even if it is someone we barely know, we should just take the time to listen to them. If we do those things, how much might it do for these people? Just think: what if you were the one hurting? Would you want someone to listen to you or at least just check in on you? I know one of the hardest things in the world is to go through difficult times alone. To close this chapter, I think this verse would be appropriate:

Eph 2:4 But because of his great love for us, God, who is rich in mercy, Eph 2:5 made us alive with Christ even when we were dead in transgressions—it is by grace you have been saved.

Mt 5:8 Blessed are the pure in heart, for they will see God.

6.
Blessed Are the Pure in Heart

In this chapter, we are getting to the core of Jesus' message. Here we have moved away from learning how to empty ourselves, and we have moved on to what Jesus spends almost more time talking about than anything else: our hearts. While so many religionists focus on outward appearances and actions, Jesus is watching our hearts. What are our motives? Are they pure, or are they superficial?

Holiness is more than outward, external actions

I don't know how many times I've had people ask me, "Will I go to hell if I do (fill in the blank with any sin here)?" Many will ask me if this is a sin, or if that thing is a sin. Should we do this? Can I do that? Other times people will tell me how good of a person they are because they do all these wonderful "Christian" rituals. Then you have those who think they are better than everyone else because they do certain things and live a certain way. These folks are quick to point out those who do not live up to their own standards. For all of these things, Jesus has this to say:

Mt 23:25 *"Woe to you, teachers of the law and Pharisees, you hypocrites! You clean the outside of the cup and dish, but inside they are full of greed and self-indulgence.*

Mt 23:26 Blind Pharisee! First clean the inside of the cup and dish, and then the outside also will be clean.
Mt 23:27 "Woe to you, teachers of the law and Pharisees, you hypocrites! You are like whitewashed tombs, which look beautiful on the outside but on the inside are full of dead men's bones and everything unclean.

He says more, but these three verses say quite a bit. It's not what is on the outside that matters. It isn't how we look, or how we dress. It's not even about the actions and good deeds we do when people are watching. What matters is what is on the inside, our hearts. What are our motives? This question goes back to the first set of Beatitudes: our hearts can become pure when we empty ourselves and let God fill us.

What is "pure in heart"?

Many interpret this passage in a purely sexual manner by saying that pureness is the absence of lustful indulgences and sexual deviations. I agree with this; however, I don't believe pureness is limited only to sexual purity. As I mentioned above, pureness of heart should permeate our entire lives. When you think of purity, what do you think of? I think of children when I think of purity.

Mt 18:3 And he said: "I tell you the truth, unless you change and become like little children, you will never enter the kingdom of heaven.

Children are the epitome of innocence and purity. As Jesus says here, we are to become like little children. This includes becoming like children in our hearts. Children don't usually harbor hate, bitterness, jealousy, or lust; nor should we. We can give these things over to the Lord, and, by doing so, we will become pure in heart.

If you read all of Jesus' teachings, you will see he is all about the heart. Sure, what we do on the outside does matter, but the outward actions are driven by the heart. Yeah, you can do good stuff with an unclean heart, but eventually your true colors will show. This is why we must empty ourselves, let God fill us with his spirit and his love, and let our hearts become pure, like those of little children. Once we do this, then we will see God.

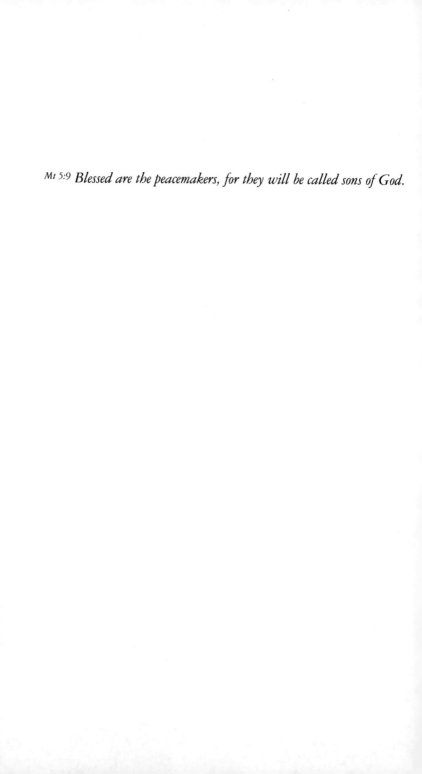

Mt 5:9 Blessed are the peacemakers, for they will be called sons of God.

7.

Blessed Are the Peacemakers

In this Beatitude, Jesus continues to call us to action. We are told to take things to the next level. We go from working on our own conditions to helping others with theirs. This is not an easy task. While we need not be perfect to be able to help others, its doesn't hurt to have a few things in order. I believe it is no accident that Jesus included peacemakers in the Beatitudes.

What is a peacemaker?

Now, I know an initial response to this question might be, "One who makes peace." However, there seems to be more to the word than that. We live in a world of conflict. Nations are constantly at war with each other; governments are continually fighting among themselves. We even see religions fighting other religions or fighting each other. Even the family isn't safe from conflict. In my work, I see kids every day who come from broken, divided, and even non-existent families. So with all this going on, how can one be a peacemaker? What even constitutes a peacemaker in the midst of all this?

Peacemaking is more than just preventing war or conflicts. It goes much deeper than that. Peacemaking is working within a world of conflict, greed, and self-centeredness while using love, compassion, and mercy to unite others before God. Paul gives some good insight on peacemaking:

Eph 4:3 *Make every effort to keep the unity of the Spirit through the bond of peace.*

Sometimes we create our own divisions for no apparent reason. For example, this book isn't about prophecy or pre-, post-, or mid-tribulation rapture. There are a variety of doctrines on this teaching, and each person through prayer and studying God's word must come to his or her own conclusion. Ultimately, having correct end times doctrine is not a requirement for salvation. Yet so often we want to make it so.

I've seen churches divide over interpretations of Revelation. While I won't get into my own view on that subject in this book, I just want to say that we need to pick and choose carefully which things we want to become dogmatic about. While it's okay to have strong feelings toward a given doctrine such as this, it's important not to condemn a brother or sister who has not come to the same understanding. Their difference on this issue doesn't make them any less of a Christian or any less holy. It simply means they have a different understanding of certain scriptures. That goes for end times teaching, young or old earth creation, and several other doctrines. These teachings by themselves are not bad. It is we that tend to cause the problems. Being able to overcome this is a huge step towards peacemaking.

Peace is a high priority goal

Paul tells us in Romans:

Ro 12:18 *If it is possible, as far as it depends on you, live at peace with everyone.*

Now, he does say, "if possible." I know sometimes there are some people who simply will not allow peace. In those instances, we must prayerfully consider our next actions. In the rest of this passage, Paul goes on to talk about feeding your enemies if they are hungry or giving them something to drink if they are thirsty. While the "if possible" sounds like it's giving us an out, Paul puts even more responsibilities on us in verses 19-20. We are to make our best efforts at all times to make peace. If a situation is not going to be peaceful, let the cause of the unrest be on others, but not on us.

Sons of God

So what did Jesus mean when saying peacemakers will be called sons of God? It would seem he means that when people see us making peace with others despite difficult circumstances, they will know that we are children of God.

Gal 3:26 *You are all sons of God through faith in Christ Jesus,*
Gal 3:27 *for all of you who were baptized into Christ have clothed yourselves with Christ.*

Our faith and love should be lived out in such a way that peacefulness will follow us. These things will be the evidence of our devotion to Jesus Christ. I can think of many times where doing that one thing to make peace broke some serious bonds. Our efforts may not even seem like a big deal to us, but, to someone else, they might make all the difference.

Here is a little story. I'll try not to put too many personal stories in here because I have a professor who hates it when preachers and teachers talk about themselves. At least he's not grading this. Almost a year ago, we still owed money on a loan we had through a local bank. I think it was for some fancy, overpriced water-softener system we had bought. We'd had this loan for several years, paying on it for what seemed like forever. Well, we'd missed a payment at some point, and we were getting these automated collection calls.

So I called them to straighten it out. It turns out I had made a payment, and they hadn't posted it yet, but they were still calling me. So I argued with the lady on the phone and even got pretty rude with her. These calls were coming in at all hours of the day, so my patience was rather thin. I yelled at this lady for a while, then hung up and called my bank. I had my bank call this bank to tell them the money had been paid from my account.

I didn't hear anything for a week or so, and I figured everything was all taken care of. Then, one day, the calls started back up. So I called that lady back, who told me, "Yes, we did get that payment, but you're still behind a payment." Now this just sent me through the roof. We were dealing with some medical bills and other expenses; it wasn't as if we had extra money to throw around. I know this doesn't excuse it, but I felt like bill collectors were ganging up on me or something. Unfortunately, I took it out on this poor woman and really let her have it over the phone.

A few weeks after that, our tax return came. I was going to send in our refund to pay off the rest of that loan, but there was a check in my spirit. I stopped and prayed, while God reminded me of how I had treated that lady on the phone. I decided instead to go to the actual bank and pay her in person. However, I did make a little stop on the way there. I stopped at a store and bought her a small little spring bouquet of flowers, nothing fancy. When I go to the bank, I sat down at her desk and apologized for my behavior. As I did so, I reached into the bag and took out the flowers. I thought she was going to faint.

At first, she looked more embarrassed than anything. She couldn't stop giggling. After she settled down, she just chatted up a storm. We had a nice little conversation. The tension that was there when I walked in was completely gone. We were no longer in bondage to whatever bitterness there had been between us. Granted, I could have avoided this whole thing, and I don't share this story to lift myself up as some great example. I should know when to keep my mouth shut. I just wanted to show how God can use a tough situation for good. In the meantime, God taught me an important lesson about being a peacemaker.

Mt 5:10 *Blessed are those who are persecuted because of righteousness,*
for theirs is the kingdom of heaven.
Mt 5:11 *"Blessed are you when people insult you, persecute you and*
falsely say all kinds of evil against you because of me.
Mt 5:12 *Rejoice and be glad, because great is your reward in heaven,*
for in the same way they persecuted the prophets who were before you.

8.
Blessed Are the Persecuted

Here we begin the last of the Beatitudes. I combined these verses since they are all describing persecution. Jesus blesses those who are persecuted for his sake. I find it interesting that he mentions persecution right after blessing the peacemakers. This would lead me to believe that we are to make peace, even in the face of persecution. As we go through life, and as we follow Jesus, we will face different levels of persecution. Some might suffer actual physical harm, perhaps even death. Most of us, however, will just be ridiculed or called names. Either way, Jesus tells us how to deal with persecution.

Persecution can follow the pursuit of righteousness

I'm sure we remember this verse:

Mt 5:6 Blessed are those who hunger and thirst for righteousness, for they will be filled.

I believe it is no accident that Jesus put both statements in his opening. We are blessed if we hunger for righteousness, even though we may suffer here on earth. Why, you may ask? I could go and give some drawn out, theological answer. The simple answer is that we live in a fallen world that is wicked and filled with sin. Men who don't know God hate the things that are of God.

When people see us behaving differently, responding differently to hard times, or just living in a different way with love and thanksgiving; they will think we are weird. I've had people tell me that plenty of times. They say I'm too easy going, or that I don't get angry enough. I've been told I have no emotions because I don't get riled up easily. Some co-workers have said I need to be more assertive and not afraid to run some people over to get ahead. The problem is, that is not God's way. People who do not know Christ (and even some who do, or who claim to) just don't get it. Unfortunately, it is all too human to fear and then to ridicule those things we do not understand. A true follower of Christ can and should be misunderstood by the world.

We should rejoice in our suffering

I know what you're probably thinking: "Why should we rejoice in suffering?" Jesus says it himself in Matthew 5:12. As he says, our reward in heaven is great for suffering here for him. Now, I don't know exactly what that reward is, but any reward given by Jesus has to be a good one. It's so easy for us to want to get down on ourselves or even to run and hide when we are ridiculed for our faith. That is often because our focus is off center. We want to think in worldly terms, in physical terms. Instead, we need to look at things in a spiritual sense. Here are the words of a missionary:

"He is no fool who gives what he cannot keep, to gain what he cannot lose."

This was found in the journal of the late Jim Elliot. He was a missionary who was murdered by the very people he was witnessing to in Ecuador in the 1950s. I believe his statement is related to this verse:

Mt 10:39 Whoever finds his life will lose it, and whoever loses his life for my sake will find it.

This idea kind of goes against the popular self-actualization teachings of American culture, doesn't it? I don't think either of them was saying we should recklessly go out of our way to endanger our lives. I know Jim Elliot had gone through a very long prayer and confirmation process before going out on his mission work. However, our problem is often much simpler. We love our lives too much. We love our lifestyles and being comfortable. I think the meaning of this verse could be as simple as saying that we should get out of our comfort zones to do God's work, instead of just playing it safe all the time. At the very least, this verse is something to pray over.

You are not the first to go through this

Jesus tells us that the prophets before us were persecuted. We know John the Baptist was beheaded. Daniel was thrown to the lions, although he survived. Elijah ran for his life many times. Then you have the apostles, only one of whom was not killed for his faith, and that was John. Even he died while in exile for preaching the gospel. After the apostles, you have about three centuries of persecution by the Roman empire. The early church suffered some of the most unspeakable acts for claiming Christ.

All of these people were serious people of God, and the world still came after them full force on many occasions. If they were not exempt, then neither are we. So when we go through these things, we know God is not picking on us but is simply refining and conforming us through trials in the way he has done to other Christians throughout history.

PART 2
Following the "Rules"

Mt 5:13 "*You are the salt of the earth. But if the salt loses its saltiness, how can it be made salty again? It is no longer good for anything, except to be thrown out and trampled by men.*
Mt 5:14 "*You are the light of the world. A city on a hill cannot be hidden.*
Mt 5:15 *Neither do people light a lamp and put it under a bowl. Instead they put it on its stand, and it gives light to everyone in the house.*
Mt 5:16 *In the same way, let your light shine before men, that they may see your good deeds and praise your Father in heaven.*

9.

The Salt and the Light

Now we move along from the Beatitudes to the next part of Jesus' sermon. In this passage, Jesus calls his people the salt and the light. During this time, salt was one of the premier spices and the most commonly used preservative. People didn't have coolers or refrigerators, so salt was quite valuable. Thus, after telling us how to empty ourselves and to be filled with God, Jesus tells us we are the salt and the light. When I was a kid growing up in church, I often heard this term thrown around, but I never really knew what it meant. In this chapter, we will see if we can figure that out.

We are the salt of the earth

As I mentioned above, salt was one of the most valuable spices and preservatives around. Like salt, followers of Jesus are the premier spice of the earth. By living for Christ and sharing his message of love throughout the world, we give the world flavor. We season it; we preserve it. If we lose our flavor, what good are we? We are of no use to the kingdom.

If we declare the name of Jesus, but do not live up to the flavor, then what will the world think of us? Have you ever wanted the ketchup, but grabbed the hot sauce instead? Here you had your mouth all set for the taste of ketchup, only to be shocked by the burning flavor of the hot sauce. You were expecting one thing, but you got another. This is what we do as Christians when we claim to be Christians but don't walk our talk. The world expects one thing, but it gets something else entirely, and that usually leaves a bad taste in people's mouths.

We are lights to the world

Here Jesus is basically re-wording the salt analogy to emphasize his point. The world is a dark place. There is war, crime, disease, famine, and death. Jesus has sent his Spirit among us to go into the world and show his love. We are to shine the light we have in our lives to the rest of the world. When we do so, others can be drawn into that light, while darkness flees the light.

I'm sure most of us have seen cockroaches. When I was in the Marines, my bathroom in our barracks was infested with cockroaches. I would turn on the bathroom light at night and see hundreds of roaches scattering and running for cover. Why is that? Because cockroaches hate the light. They live in darkness and fear the light. Before I was a Christian, this was how I lived. I enjoyed things that were evil and sinful and grew angry and fearful anytime someone threatened those things.

Sin hates the light. When we go into the world, into the dark places, and let our lights shine, then the sin and evil scatters. It might put up a fight at first, but that is only because of fear, which also hates the light. We keep the light shining and the darkness will flee, just like the cockroaches. Unfortunately, most of us are content to sit in our cozy pews at church, hoping someone else will be the ones shining that light.

Let our lights shine to all

When those who don't know Christ see our good deeds, or

when we help them for what seems like no reason whatsoever, they will probably want to know why. I'm not saying we should tell them we will do X if they do Y. One thing I've seen many Christians and churches do is to do a good deed for someone, such as shoveling their driveway in a snowstorm or mowing their lawn, and then coming to that person and saying, "Since we did this for you, we'd like you to listen to what we have to share." I'm sorry, but I don't agree with this. True kindness comes with no strings attached.

When we show love and compassion to others and expect nothing in return, that is when true seeds are sown. People will want to know why we are helping them and what we want. Why do we seem joyful even when things aren't going so well? I've had people ask me this many times. That doesn't mean if we are going through hard times, we need to put on a happy face and pretend all is well. On the same note, we always have a feeling of hope when we are going through dark times that we don't have without Christ. Shining our light on people who do not know Christ will open up doors. It will create situations in which we can dialogue. It is during those times that we can share with them the hope we have in Jesus Christ.

Mt 5:17 "Do not think that I have come to abolish the Law or the Prophets; I have not come to abolish them but to fulfill them. *Mt 5:18* I tell you the truth, until heaven and earth disappear, not the smallest letter, not the least stroke of a pen, will by any means disappear from the Law until everything is accomplished. *Mt 5:19* Anyone who breaks one of the least of these commandments and teaches others to do the same will be called least in the kingdom of heaven, but whoever practices and teaches these commands will be called great in the kingdom of heaven.

Mt 5:20 For I tell you that unless your righteousness surpasses that of the Pharisees and the teachers of the law, you will certainly not enter the kingdom of heaven.

10.
The Fulfillment of the Law

In this passage, Jesus begins to discuss the law of Moses. This is what the Jews had lived by up until this point. Jesus refers to both the law and prophets, so it's probably safe to assume he is referring to the Septuagint, which is basically the Greek translation of the Old Testament. That was the version of the scriptures they most likely had at this time.

When looking at Jesus' words, some believe he is stating that we must follow all laws of the Old Testament to this very day. They would insist that we are still to follow the law to the letter. Yet many say that we are no longer under the law. So which is it? In this chapter, we will see if we can't figure that out.

Jesus did not come to abolish the law

I will try to keep this as simple as I can. As I said in the beginning, this book is not intended as an academic study for theologians, but as a practical guide for our daily lives. Volumes have been written on this topic, so for more in-depth reading on this, just do a Google search on "Sermon on the Mount" and "Law," and you'll find more than you'll ever want to read.

First we must ask, "What did Jesus mean by fulfilling the law?" If we go all the way back to Genesis, we may discover part of the answer:

TIM MILLER

Ge 3:15 *And I will put enmity between you and the woman, and between your offspring and hers; he will crush your head, and you will strike his heel.*

This is one of the first prophecies of the coming of Jesus. God tells the serpent (Satan) that the offspring of the woman (Jesus) will crush his head. Jesus did just that by dying on the cross for our sins. Genesis 3 describes the fall of man. From that point forward, everything in the Bible including the law is setting the stage for the coming of Christ. Even the Passover in Exodus and the sacrificial system in Leviticus symbolizes Christ. So, in his death, he fulfilled the purpose of the ceremonial laws. The book of Hebrews explains this in beautiful detail.

Part of Jesus' desire here was to clarify the purpose of the law. The Pharisees and religious leaders at the time had burdened the people with such a heavy, legalistic load. They were suffocating spiritually. Jesus wanted to show us the spirit of the law and not just the letter. After all, Jesus did also say this:

Mt 11:30 *For my yoke is easy and my burden is light.*

So if our burden is heavy and our yoke is too hard, then perhaps we should re-think exactly who it is we're following. Are we following Jesus, or man's religious systems?

Until heaven and earth disappear

In verse 18, Jesus includes a key phrase in his statement. That phrase is, "Until all is accomplished." What was he talking about? Did he mean until the end of the world? He says something similar here:

Mt 24:35 Heaven and earth will pass away, but my words will never pass away.

I'm not going to get into too much detail about Matthew 24; however, when Jesus says, "until all things are accomplished" in chapter 5, it would seem, knowing what we know now, that he is referring to his own death and resurrection. What does he mean when he refers to heaven and earth passing away? It almost sounds like a figure of speech, kind of like when someone says, "Come hell or high water, I won't give up!" They don't literally mean hell or high water is on its way. Jesus was trying to show how certain it was that his words would not pass away and that his mission would be accomplished. That is not to say we don't take Jesus' words literally. The point of this passage is about heaven and earth passing away. It's about Jesus fulfilling the Law.

The purpose of the Old Testament sacrifices and many of the laws were to cover men's sins. When Jesus died and rose again, he became the perfect and permanent sacrifice. Not only did he fulfill the law and major themes of the Old Testament, but Jesus also fulfilled every minor prophecy about himself. This is what he likely meant when he said, "Not the smallest letter, not the least stroke of a pen, will by any means disappear from the law until everything is accomplished." He wasn't just here to fulfill the big things, but all the minor details as well.

Righteousness must surpass that of the Pharisees

Here Jesus hits his main point by jabbing his finger into the eye of the Pharisees. There seems to be a bit of sarcasm here as well. The Pharisees were rich and proud. They followed the letter of the law and loathed sinners or anyone who could not measure up to their standards, which was most people. They did not seem to believe in grace or mercy. To them, once you sinned, you were a sinner and of no use to anyone. Jesus was telling us to be better than this by obeying his commands and being humble. To Jesus, obeying the law is not just a superficial fulfillment of outward actions. It is obedience with a humble and loving heart.

Law and grace are two things that must strike a balance. Some churches teach nothing but strict adherence to the law. Others teach what is often called "cheap grace," or the idea that there is no need to change one's heart or actions, but that all is forgiven no matter what you do, and so there is no need to do much of anything. This passage offers a balance between these two extremes. Following God's moral laws with love and humility is necessary as we fellowship with him in our daily walk. This is another way we may show the world that we are the salt and the light. One thing I will probably mention over and over in this book is this: *Discipleship is more than outward actions.* You will see that phrase again.

Mt 5:21 *You have heard that it was said to the people long ago, 'Do not murder, and anyone who murders will be subject to judgment.'*
Mt 5:22 *But I tell you that anyone who is angry with his brother will be subject to judgment. Again, anyone who says to his brother, 'Raca,' is answerable to the Sanhedrin. But anyone who says, 'You fool!' will be in danger of the fire of hell.*
Mt 5:23 *Therefore, if you are offering your gift at the altar and there remember that your brother has something against you,*
Mt 5:24 *leave your gift there in front of the altar. First go and be reconciled to your brother; then come and offer your gift.*
Mt 5:25 *Settle matters quickly with your adversary who is taking you to court. Do it while you are still with him on the way, or he may hand you over to the judge, and the judge may hand you over to the officer, and you may be thrown into prison.*
Mt 5:26 *I tell you the truth, you will not get out until you have paid the last penny.*

11.
Thou Shalt Not Kill?

In this chapter, we come to Matthew 5:21-26 (above). In this passage, Jesus repeats the commandment to not commit murder. However, he seems to take the command a step farther here. He says not only are we not to commit murder, but we are not to be angry with each other. We are to resolve our disputes among ourselves before going before the Judge. What exactly is he talking about? Let's break this passage down and see if we can't figure it out.

The 10 Commandments say, "Thou shalt not kill."

Jesus simply repeats this command in verse twenty-one. The Jews and Pharisees seemed to follow this pretty well. They thought they were doing okay. They figured, "Hey, I made it through today without killing anyone. I'm holy!" Not so fast. I mentioned above that discipleship is more than just an outward act of obedience. So what is going on here?

First, I should clear something up. The NIV translation as used in this book used the word "murder." The King James and some others use the word "kill." Some believe the use of the word "murder" narrows the definition to a specific kind of killing. That is possible, but Jesus didn't stop at that interpretation.

But I tell you…

Jesus says that anyone who is angry with his brother and says, "You fool!" is subject to judgment. The term "raca" also appears in this passage. In Aramaic, it means about the same thing as "you fool." Jesus tells us that one who says such things is in danger of the fires of hell. This is serious stuff. One could argue that Jesus is talking about having an argument with someone, but this passage appears to imply much more than just angry words. We can see this from the next thing he says.

Be reconciled to your brother

Jesus discusses giving sacrifices and says to make sure you are reconciled to your brother before making such a sacrifice. Do you notice how he puts the religious ritual on hold in order to mend relationships between people? The act appears subtle here, but it is huge! How many times do we just go to church and go about our business while harboring bitterness or hatred toward one of our brothers or sister? Jesus says to forget all that. Forget church and forget Wednesday night Bible study. Get out there and reconcile with your brother. Now, if they refuse to reconcile, that is another thing, and the responsibility is no longer on you. You tried. But relationships come before religion.

Also, Jesus doesn't want us coming before him with hatred and bitterness in our hearts. Hatred and bitterness do nothing but keep us in bondage. How much bondage? Enough that Jesus basically equates harboring those negative feelings with killing someone. That is what I get from this passage. When you hate your brother, you have killed him in your heart, which means you have killed in God's eyes. Remember, discipleship is more than outward acts. When we go to God and ask him for forgiveness, how can he forgive us, when we haven't even forgiven others?

Settle matters with your adversary

Even if we are being sued, Jesus says to settle matters before they get to court. We could spiritualize this as well. Jesus could be referring to settling things with our enemies on earth, in our hearts, before we face Jesus as judge. He could also literally mean to settle things with our literal adversary who is literally suing us in a literal court.

Now, if the person is just bound and determined to push things as far as they will go, then you just can't settle. But once again, the issue is then no longer your responsibility. You tried and you obeyed, but your opponent refuses to back down. However, we also know all things are possible through Christ. In such a situation, we would be best served spending as much time in prayer as possible and placing the matter in his hands.

This is a tough lesson. We are now past the fluff. As we get deeper into the Sermon on the Mount, Christ's teaching gets tougher. As we read these words, we need prayerfully to ask God to guide us through this study and to reveal his truths in our lives. The words will become harsher; the lessons will grow tougher, and none of us will get a pass.

Mt 5:27 *You have heard that it was said, 'Do not commit adultery.'*
Mt 5:28 *But I tell you that anyone who looks at a woman lustfully has already committed adultery with her in his heart.*
Mt 5:29 *If your right eye causes you to sin, gouge it out and throw it away. It is better for you to lose one part of your body than for your whole body to be thrown into hell.*
Mt 5:30 *And if your right hand causes you to sin, cut it off and throw it away. It is better for you to lose one part of your body than for your whole body to go into hell.*

12.

Adultery: More Than Sexual?

In the above passage, Jesus reviews the commandment about not committing adultery. He clarifies the command and once again expands it. I've been saying he "expands it," but I suppose that's not actually the best way to describe it. What he's really doing is clarifying the commands by explaining their original meaning, which is not the same as the religious leaders' interpretations of them. When Jesus does this, it does not please the Pharisees. They thought they had a pretty good understanding of the law, since they had been teaching it. They sure didn't like this Jesus fellow coming along and making life tougher on them. Once again, Jesus shows that obedience to God means more than just outward appearances of holiness.

Adultery is more than a physical act

Jesus drops a bomb in this passage. He says, "Sure, the law says not to commit adultery, but I tell you"—notice the authority with which he speaks—that even lusting after a woman in your heart is adultery. Wow. Now there are a couple of things to clarify here. At this time, the Jewish culture had a very narrow view of what constituted adultery. They pretty much limited it to sleeping with a married woman. So if a man was married and he slept with a prostitute, at that time it was not considered adultery. This was just how they did things back then. So, understandably, when Jesus tells them not even to lust, they were upset at their fun being spoiled.

Lust is an issue with which so many people struggle. Even among Christians, so many men battle this temptation daily. There are women who struggle with it as well. Sexuality is played up so much in the media and in society. We are bombarded constantly with sexual images. Sex almost seems like no big deal anymore. To some, it's a recreational sport like golf. Yet, here, Jesus is telling us to keep our minds pure of such thoughts. This is not an easy task, but it is one that is possible.

First, I think we need to clarify Jesus' intent here. This passage, like many, gets used and abused. As I mentioned earlier, Jesus was addressing the much larger problem of married men sleeping with prostitutes (among other things they were doing). Therefore, when he's talking about lusting, he's concerned about intent. What is your intent in looking at that woman? For example, if I look at porn on my computer, then it's safe to say I'm not looking to admire women as godly creations.

On the other hand, many churches have taught that if you look at a woman wearing a short skirt and find her attractive, then you must instantly burn your eyes out of their sockets. Okay, so I'm exaggerating, but just a little. I know what you're thinking. "Jesus said to pluck out your eye if it offends you." Yes, he did, and that is my next point.

Remove those things that cause you to sin

I don't believe Jesus is saying that we literally need to gouge out our eyes or lop off our hands. I do believe he is saying if you struggle with lust, then you need to prevent it. For example, if you struggle with looking at porn on the computer, then get filters for your computer, accountability software, or maybe even get rid of the computer for a time. If you struggle with inappropriate shows on TV, block out those stations you are tempted by, or, if that doesn't work, get rid of the TV altogether.

I've known some folks with sexual addictions who have come to me and told me, "Man, I'm really feeling the urge to act out sexually." But when I look at the music they listen to, it's all stuff about sticking it here, rubbing it there, girls singing about their "humps," "milkshakes," and "goodies." If that's all I listened to, then I would probably be fixated on sex too.

I'm not saying we must all listen to nothing but Christian music and watch nothing but church shows and Veggie Tales. I'm saying if we struggle in this area, then each of us needs to examine our lives and remove those things that cause us to stumble. I'm not exempt from this myself. I've had my own struggles over the years. We've put porn filters on our computer as well. While it filters out most of the bad stuff, occasionally something gets through that's questionable.

I know when doing my online ministry on MySpace, I have to be very careful. So far, so good though. Even though there is a lot of garbage on sites like MySpace, there are a lot of wonderful Christians, and a lot of hurting people just looking for someone to reach out to them. It is a place ripe for ministry. One thing I have learned over the last several years when it comes to dealing with lust is that God would rather we learn to handle our urges than just take them away completely.

Sexuality is a gift from God. It is one of the most beautiful gifts he has given us. It is man that has corrupted and cheapened it. We have stamped it on a lunch box and put it up for sale. This is not what God intended. I remember my teenage years when I attended a Baptist church. I used to pray for hours each day for God to take my sexual desires away. My body was changing, and I had no idea what to do about it. Over the years, I've known men who were told by their pastors to never ever to talk to any woman that was not their wife.

That all sounds good in theory, but it's just not realistic. Women are God's creation, too, and they happen to make up a large part of the planet. They also make up a majority of churchgoers. Women are not the problem. It's what men formulate in their head that is the problem. God doesn't want us to hide from what he has given us. Women are a precious gift from God and can bless us in many non-sexual ways. God would rather we learn to use his gifts in the correct way than pretend they don't exist. God can help us through this struggle if we let him. It might not be easy, and it might take some time. All we need to do is surrender to his perfect will and put him first in our lives. Once again, it's that discipleship thing. More than just outward actions.

Mt 5:31 It has been said, 'Anyone who divorces his wife must give her a certificate of divorce.'

Mt 5:32 But I tell you that anyone who divorces his wife, except for marital unfaithfulness, causes her to become an adulteress, and anyone who marries the divorced woman commits adultery.

13.
When Is Divorce Justified?

This passage covers another tough lesson from Jesus. In Matthew 5:31-32, he talks about divorce and when it is allowed. The first thing we need to do here is to establish some background for this passage. During Christ's time, divorce was rather common. However, only men could initiate a divorce. Jewish law and customs at the time allowed men to divorce their wives for just about anything. Tradition tells us a man could divorce his wife for burning his dinner! Now, there weren't a whole lot of waitressing jobs or secretarial schools for women to attend back then, so divorced women often ended up working as prostitutes just to survive. So Jesus wanted to clarify the command here to show what God actually intended.

Divorce was allowed as long as a certificate was given

In this passage, Jesus talks about what had been allowed previously. He elaborates later in chapter 19.

Mt 19:8 Jesus replied, "Moses permitted you to divorce your wives because your hearts were hard. But it was not this way from the beginning.

So early on there was an allowance made for divorce, but Jesus says that it was never intended to be that way. Matthew 19:1-11 has more detail for further reading. The main thing is what Jesus says in Matthew 19:8: "Because your hearts were hard." That is the key right there. God set up marriage in a perfect way. It was we men who messed it all up.

Divorce was justified in cases of adultery

Some translations say "fornication." The Greek word used here is "porneia," which at the time was a generic term for sexual sin. It could be used interchangeably with adultery or fornication or anything else sexual, so it wasn't a limited context. The Apostle Paul expands on this as well:

1Co 7:10 To the married I give this command (not I, but the Lord): A wife must not separate from her husband.
1Co 7:11 But if she does, she must remain unmarried or else be reconciled to her husband. And a husband must not divorce his wife.

This passage often leads to some contention. Paul says in verse 10 above that "a wife must not separate from her husband." This sounds pretty clear until the next sentence when he says, "..but if she does…" This would lead one to believe that there is some kind of allowance being made. Some believe he's referring to Jesus' command about committing sexual sin, but there is no reference to that here. Paul continues:

1Co 7:12 To the rest I say this (I, not the Lord): If any brother has a wife who is not a believer and she is willing to live with him, he must not divorce her.
1Co 7:13 And if a woman has a husband who is not a believer and he is willing to live with her, she must not divorce him.
1Co 7:14 For the unbelieving husband has been sanctified through his wife, and the unbelieving wife has been sanctified through her believing

husband. Otherwise your children would be unclean, but as it is, they are holy.

1Co 7:15 But if the unbeliever leaves, let him do so. A believing man or woman is not bound in such circumstances; God has called us to live in peace.

Paul says here that if we are married to unbelievers, we must not leave them just because they are unbelievers. However, if they choose to leave us, then we are not bound to them. Many believe this means we are free to remarry since the marriage was not binding. It is also a common belief that if your spouse commits adultery, that the marriage bond is broken and the offended spouse is free to remarry. Is anyone confused yet?

Here is where things get sticky. Many people have often asked me about abusive marriages. I'm not sure how much of a problem this was in the first century, to be honest, but what if the husband is physically, emotionally, verbally, or sexually abusive to his wife? Or even vice versa? Is divorce allowed in such cases?

This is not an easy question at all. Some would say it's an easy one; they just point to the adultery passage and say, "See! This is the only reason given right there!" Technically, that's correct. There was a church near us a few years ago that a friend of mine used to attend. A woman in this church was in an abusive marriage for quite awhile. One day, her husband beat her severely, nearly killing her. She had several broken bones and spent weeks in the hospital. When she was well enough, she got a restraining order against him and filed for divorce.

Back at her church, the husband was allowed to return after getting bailed out of jail. The wife, however, was told by the pastor that unless she could prove that he was cheating on her, that she did not have biblical grounds for divorce. He told her abuse was not mentioned anywhere in the Bible as grounds for divorce; therefore, she was to reunite with her husband. When she refused, she was kicked out of the church for leaving the man who had almost killed her. Now, I've been accused of being too liberal on this issue, but I don't think Jesus meant this command to be so narrow.

Once again, let's go back to the beginning of this sermon. Remember Jesus' theme: Obedience is more than external actions. His focus throughout the gospels is the condition of one's heart. He said that lusting after another woman is committing adultery. He said hating your brother is the same as murder. So are we seeing a pattern here? Based on what we've seen Jesus talk about with regard to the spirit of the law and the letter, we need to ask some hard questions. Is it really a godly thing to continue living with a spouse who cannot stand you, who doesn't talk to you or touch you, who hits you, degrades you, or wants nothing to do with you or the children?

I'm not going to get into all the qualities of godly marriages here. You could write a whole book just on marriage, and many have. I'm just trying to point out what the Bible tells us and what Jesus taught. This requires some tough questions. I myself don't have the answers to all of them. I know in my work and ministry, I have come across many victims of abuse. In those cases, I don't tell them what they should do. I pray with them and ask God to tell them. No matter what, I always err on the side of grace and mercy as opposed to religion and condemnation.

I want to make clear here that I am in no way encouraging divorce. God hates divorce, and it is in no way a decision that should be taken lightly or come upon casually. However, we are not perfect and neither are our spouses. Sometimes we end up in situations that are beyond our control, and all we can do is turn to God and pray for his mercy and restoration.

Mt 5:33 *Again, you have heard that it was said to the people long ago, 'Do not break your oath, but keep the oaths you have made to the Lord.'*

Mt 5:34 *But I tell you, Do not swear at all: either by heaven, for it is God's throne;*

Mt 5:35 *or by the earth, for it is his footstool; or by Jerusalem, for it is the city of the Great King.*

Mt 5:36 *And do not swear by your head, for you cannot make even one hair white or black.*

Mt 5:37 *Simply let your 'Yes' be 'Yes,' and your 'No,' 'No'; anything beyond this comes from the evil one.*

14.

Do You Swear to Tell the Truth?

ere Jesus gives us commands on swearing oaths. This seems rather uneventful after all the talk about gouging out eyes and lopping off limbs. However, it's something that is obviously important. This passage has been interpreted in many different ways. In the Old Testament law, Moses commanded us to abide by any oaths we swear. Here, Jesus says to swear no oaths. So is Jesus contradicting Moses? I don't think so. If we take a look at Jesus' words, and the whole of scripture, we can see he was simply clarifying Moses' original command.

The law said to keep our oaths

Dt 6:13 Fear the LORD your God, serve him only and take your oaths in his name.
Dt 6:14 Do not follow other gods, the gods of the peoples around you;

This is what Moses tells us in regard to swearing oaths. He said if you swear an oath, to do so in the Lord's name. So was Jesus telling us something different? I often hear people saying things like, "I swear to God!" I'm not sure that's the type of oath to which this passage refers. Perhaps a better example of what is intended is when someone places his hand over a Bible and swears to tell the truth. Granted, they didn't have Bibles back then, but I'm sure an oath wasn't something that was taken casually, at least not at first.

Jesus said to swear no oaths

Many have taken this passage in Matthew to mean that we should never swear any oaths at all, under any circumstances whatsoever. This would include taking an oath in a court of law, or being sworn in for a government job. You could even put marriage vows in the mix depending on how legalistic you wanted to become over it. However, this is not what Jesus meant.

One problem we have in today's society is the absence of truth. We live in a world that believes there is no such thing as absolute moral truth, or any truth at all for that matter. Even if you enter into an agreement with someone and sign a legal contract, people will still try to challenge it. Look at the divorce rate. Yes, we covered some reasons one could divorce, but a great many divorces are not for those reasons. Yet, we back out of our vows or contracts as if they meant nothing. Today, a person's word is practically worthless.

So what was Jesus saying?

For one, he was touching on this commandment:

Ex 20:7 You shall not misuse the name of the LORD your God, for the LORD will not hold anyone guiltless who misuses his name.

Jesus was reminding us, for one, not to take the name of the Lord in vain. It always amazes me how many people claim they don't believe in Jesus and yet want to shout his name whenever they are angry. However, taking the Lord's name in vain isn't just using his name to curse. Jesus was also emphasizing how important our word is and how it should not be thrown around lightly. During Christ's time, men would swear oaths to each other in business deals with no intention of following through on their obligations.

Heb 6:16 Men swear by someone greater than themselves, and the oath confirms what is said and puts an end to all argument.

Once again, we need to consider the whole of scripture, and Hebrews does not condemn taking oaths. It tells us, instead, what strength an oath in the name of the Lord has. We know how much the Pharisees twisted scripture at this time. They would contort the law to suit their own purposes. Much like today, people will swear to anything, only to go back on their word as soon as something better comes along. One thing the Pharisees were known for was swearing oaths by anything but God. The reason they did this was so that when they went back on their word, they wouldn't be accountable to God, at least in their minds.

So after examining the whole of scripture, we see that Jesus is reminding us not to take the Lord's name in vain and only to give an oath in serious matters. God's name is holy and pure. It's not something to throw around casually. Neither is our good word. When we make a promise, people should be able to count on that promise, especially when we claim the name of Jesus Christ as our savior.

Mt 5:38 *You have heard that it was said,*
'Eye for eye, and tooth for tooth.'
Mt 5:39 *But I tell you, Do not resist an evil person. If someone strikes*
you on the right cheek, turn to him the other also.
Mt 5:40 *And if someone wants to sue you and take your tunic,*
let him have your cloak as well.
Mt 5:41 *If someone forces you to go one mile, go with him two miles.*
Mt 5:42 *Give to the one who asks you, and do not turn away*
from the one who wants to borrow from you.

15.
An Eye for an Eye

This is one of the most talked about and most controversial passages in the Bible. Many of us have trouble understanding this passage. As with the rest of the Sermon on the Mount, we must look at what Jesus is saying, what it meant to his original audience, and what it means today. Some have taken this passage to mean that we are not to resist any form of evil or violence in any way, shape, or form, under any circumstances. Others take a bit looser approach and say he was speaking completely figuratively. So which is it? In this chapter, we will attempt to answer these questions.

An eye for an eye, or do not resist?

First, we should take a look at the book of Exodus and view the law itself.

Ex 21:23 But if there is serious injury, you are to take life for life,
Ex 21:24 eye for eye, tooth for tooth, hand for hand, foot for foot,
Ex 21:25 burn for burn, wound for wound, bruise for bruise.

Yet what Jesus commands sounds like just the opposite of this Exodus passage. Why is that? A couple of things are going on here. When this part of the law was given in Exodus, we must remember that Israel was a new nation. They had no laws. They were a theocracy ruled only by God. God gave these laws so they would have some social order. Such laws were to be enforced by the authorities that God had put into place. This was the original purpose and spirit of the law. However, over the years, things got rather twisted. These scriptures over time became used by people to extract personal revenge for wrongs committed to them. This resulted in a bitter and vengeful society.

So when Jesus says, "do not resist and evil person," we now have some background on the purpose of the original law. He does not appear to be saying to sit by and allow an evil person to perform all sorts of evil deeds or to do physical harm to others. It also means that neither should we become vigilantes or turn to violence as our first response. Jesus tells us instead what we should do. The problem is, his solution isn't popular with many.

He told us to turn the other cheek. If a person slaps us on the cheek, instead of slapping them back, we offer them our other cheek and allow them to slap us. Now, for most of us, this makes no sense whatsoever. Our initial and human reaction is to smack them back and twice as hard! Yet, in doing that, we are missing an important lesson. The instant we offer up our other cheek to our offender, they have lost any power over us they may have had through their use of violence.

Having worked in law enforcement and corrections for many years, and because I currently work with troubled kids, I see this all the time. People resort to violence as a means of bullying or intimidation. When someone resorts to violence, it's usually because they want something. They are either looking for a fight, which will fuel their anger even more, or they are after something that belongs to you.

When you respond in kindness, this is like throwing a blanket on that fire. Their power is gone. You are not their victim any longer. They are only doing to you what you allow. The same thing is happening in verse 41. Roman soldiers in those days would make civilians carry their gear sometimes. If a soldier makes you carry his pack for a mile, go ahead and offer to carry it for an extra mile.

If someone takes something from you…give them more?

This goes back to the transfer of power. We often see these TV court shows where a person is being sued, so they go and file a counter suit. We live in a litigation happy society. People will sue over the slightest thing. I've even seen situations where Christians will sue each other over silly things. One of the saddest things I've seen is pastors suing other pastors over bad situations that have arisen in their ministry. This is not what God intended for us.

In verse 40, Jesus tells us that if someone sues us for our tunic, that we should give them our tunic *and* our cloak. Often times, when a person sues, it's to get even, to get what they think they are owed, or even to use a power or intimidation tactic. So when a person sues you for a sum of money, and you end up giving them more than they are asking for, what does that do to their feelings of revenge? Will they still feel like they've won? Maybe, maybe not. Either way, you have taken their power away from them. What you have done is told them, "Here, neither you, nor the things of this world have power over me." In these cases, Jesus is trying to help us see past our "tit-for-tat" mentality.

Now I understand that we may not have the money to do this. Perhaps we are being sued for a much larger amount of money than we actually have. I don't think Jesus is telling us that we cannot get a lawyer and defend ourselves. In the

course of defending ourselves, however, we can do so with
love and Christian understanding. We don't have to discredit
the plaintiff, or bear false witness against him just to protect
ourselves. If we're being sued over something for which we
were clearly in the wrong, then I suppose we should take up
the issue with God in prayer to determine what we should do.

Do not turn away from a borrower

In verse 42, Jesus is trying to emphasize the importance
of generosity. He's trying to tell us not to guard constantly
our money (which he gave us anyway) and not to worry always
about being fair or about things being even. He's saying go
ahead and loan someone money. If they don't pay you back,
it was never yours to begin with. Now, I know he wants us to
be good stewards and not just to give away everything he has
given to us. I've heard that argument many times. However, I
think it's safe to say that for the majority of us, that isn't going
to be a problem. Most of us Americans like our money and
will hold onto it with a death grip. Jesus wants us to hold on
to him, not our money.

So in this passage, we see that Jesus is not bogging us
down with more rules or laws; he is liberating us from worldly
norms. This does not mean we just sit there and allow someone
to beat us to a pulp. Jesus also was not implying that we should
allow someone else to be beaten up. Putting it simply, Jesus is
telling us not to retaliate, not to take our own revenge. When
placed in a conflict, the world tells us we must stand up, or be
tough and get even. Jesus says it's okay to let the other person
have his way. In order to be a committed disciple, we must free
ourselves of having our own way. One way to do this is to turn
the other cheek.

Mt 5:43 *You have heard that it was said,*
'Love your neighbor and hate your enemy.'
Mt 5:44 *But I tell you: Love your enemies and*
pray for those who persecute you,
Mt 5:45 *that you may be sons of your Father in heaven.*
He causes his sun to rise on the evil and the good,
and sends rain on the righteous and the unrighteous.
Mt 5:46 *If you love those who love you, what reward will you get?*
Are not even the tax collectors doing that?
Mt 5:47 *And if you greet only your brothers, what are you doing more*
than others? Do not even pagans do that?
Mt 5:48 *Be perfect, therefore, as your heavenly Father is perfect.*

16.
Love Your Enemies

J esus clearly tells us to love our enemies in this interesting and even controversial passage. This passage is one that, in my experience, everyone seems to know about but few seem to follow. I don't know how many times I've heard someone say, "Sure, I love my enemies." Then the second someone does them harm, they instantly begin wishing or planning ill will towards that person. I've seen so many Christians caught up in some vindictive power struggle. One Christian lady once said to me, "When Jesus said to love our enemies, he didn't mean we have to be nice to them!" Now I don't suppose we are required to have them over for Christmas dinner, but I guess your response depends on what you consider "being nice."

As I write this, our nation is still at war in Iraq. Terror still dominates our headlines, and threats of terrorist attacks seem to make the news daily. I don't intend to get into a political discussion here. However, I do want to address some things I've long found disturbing. I don't mean to be overly critical of Christians, but since I am one myself, and I do believe we are held to a higher standard, I feel it necessary to point out some problems as I see them.

I've seen so many Christians who seem to feel that we need to nuke the entire Middle East off the face of the earth, bomb Iran, or perhaps just go around the world, round up all Muslims, and put bullets in all their heads, and that will make the world's problems go away. I hope I'm not the only one who has a problem with this. You can feel what you want about war in general, or just this war, but whenever I hear such talk from fellow believers, it just makes me cringe.

The world tells us to hate our enemies

This is a pretty common attitude among many non-Christians I know. Someone is your enemy, so you do what you can to destroy them. There are a lot of neat catch phrases that tell us how to deal with our enemies. Phrases such as "The enemy of my enemy is my friend" and "Keep your friends close, but your enemies closer."

People don't say these things to get to know their enemies better. They use them as guidelines on how to destroy their enemies, whether financially, through their reputations, or even physically. The world tells us this is okay. Seek vengeance; get even; hate your enemy. I guess the question we need to ask ourselves is, "Just where and when does the hatred end?" We talked earlier about the transfer of power. How much power do we give our enemies over us when we decide to hate them?

I've known many people over the years who are completely consumed by hate. Before I was a Christian, I had a lot of hatred and bitterness in my heart. I wanted to punish those who had wronged me. I made myself physically ill thinking over and over about the wrongs people had done to me. I would fantasize about doing them harm, or destroying their lives or careers in some way. They needed to pay.

Jesus said to love our enemies

This is where people get confused. People often think that this means we must allow our enemies to step all over us and continue to harm us. Others just sort of ignore this altogether. When I read this passage, it makes me think of a recent news story. In October of 2006, a man by the name of Charles Carl Roberts IV walked into an Amish school in Lancaster County, Pennsylvania and opened fire. Four young girls were killed along with a teacher's aide. Roberts killed himself before police could close in on him.

I remember what a big story this was when it broke. However, what I remember becoming an even bigger story than the shooting itself was the fact that the Amish community had stated that they forgave the shooter. Matt Lauer on the *Today Show* seemed pretty baffled by this, as did many other media outlets. They interviewed former Amish people, and people living in and near this Amish community, and they could not understand why they would forgive this man who killed their daughters.

I heard one spokesman for the community say it this way: "They are glad it happened to their daughters, because they know they were ready to be with God. If it happened in another place, those children might not have been ready." I can't think of any other statement that shows more love than this one. How many times do we wish our tragedies on someone else? We may pray, "Oh, God, why does this have to happen to me? Why can't it happen to those sinners down the street?" These folks not only accepted this tragedy, but embraced it. They embraced it through loving their enemy, the man who murdered their children.

Loving those who love us is easy

Jesus says this in verses 46-47. Even the tax collectors and pagans love those who love them. Everyone in the world loves their friends and families. That is really not that hard to do, nor is it that big of a deal apparently. It's easy to love and care about those who love and care about you. The real question is, "Can we love the unlovable?" Jesus didn't introduce this as a rhetorical question. He was challenging us to show the same love to others that he has shown to us.

I've worked with many angry people. I had a former employer who was consumed with anger. I loved the man, and I prayed for him daily. I can't even imagine what could have been going on in his life that tortured him in such a way. He would have outbursts in the office in which he would yell, scream, and threaten to fire all of us. After several months, I finally decided I just could not work for him. I was angry, and it was hard for me to deal with that, but I did the best that I could. I just figured it was a matter of time before he fired me in the midst of one of his outbursts.

This man was very hard to love. I had to go home daily and pray and pray for God's grace and patience to not strangle this guy. When I did leave the job, I felt more sadness toward him than anger. As much as I wanted to help him, it just didn't seem like I was in a position as his subordinate to do so. However, sometimes I wonder if I may have left too quickly and if I could have handled it differently. I still pray that the Lord sends someone to him who can reach out to him. Loving the unlovable is one of the hardest things for us, even the most gentle among us, to do.

As we've seen here, it's easy to love our friends while hating our enemies. We are no different than anyone else in the world. I'm sure that the Nazis loved their friends and family. Even Saddam Hussein probably felt some love toward his sons. That is the world's standard. As I said earlier, we Christians are held to a different standard. Jesus called us to a higher standard. His standard might be much harder and more demanding than the world's, but his rewards are eternal.

PART 3
Heaven On Earth

Mt 6:1 *Be careful not to do your 'acts of righteousness' before men, to be seen by them. If you do, you will have no reward from your Father in heaven.*

Mt 6:2 *So when you give to the needy, do not announce it with trumpets, as the hypocrites do in the synagogues and on the streets, to be honored by men. I tell you the truth, they have received their reward in full.*

Mt 6:3 *But when you give to the needy, do not let your left hand know what your right hand is doing,*

Mt 6:4 *so that your giving may be in secret. Then your Father, who sees what is done in secret, will reward you*

17.
Giving to the Poor the Right Way

Giving to the poor is something that many people do or at least should do. Both Christians and non-Christians give to the poor. Many churches have ministries set up just for helping the poor. In this passage, Jesus doesn't tell us why we should give or even how much we should give to the poor. He tells us instead how to go about giving; not just about the act itself, but about where our hearts should be in the process.

There are many people who like to give and then tell the world what they've done. I've known of some churches that are raising funds for new building projects. During their fundraisers, they have a large graph in the church that grows each week to show how close they are to their goal. Some churches have gone so far as to recognize top donors in front of the congregation. I currently attend a Christian college. One thing that always baffled me is the names of people on the buildings. One professor explained to me that they name the buildings after the donors who gave the largest sums of money to build them. Isn't that the opposite of what Jesus is saying? Many of us view giving to the poor as a way to gain recognition, but Jesus is telling us something completely different.

Do not do your good deeds before men

This is the first statement Jesus makes in this passage. He isn't saying that we should avoid anyone seeing our good deeds at all costs. It's possible to become too legalistic about this command. We must look at some of the things that were going on during this time. The Pharisees and high priests would often go and make a big production of their giving. They would announce to people what they'd done, and they would make sure they got lots of praise heaped upon themselves for their good deeds.

Jesus tells us here that this is not good. In fact, making a big spectacle of our actions will cause us to lose any reward we may have had in heaven. We need to ask ourselves which is more important: praise from men, or praise from God?

Hypocrites announce their giving

Jesus took this issue so seriously that he called those who trumpeted their giving hypocrites. He calls them hypocrites because they are not actually giving in order to help someone. They are giving because they want others to see them. They make sure the entire world knows just what they gave, to whom they gave it, and how much. One thing they make sure of is that they were seen by as many as possible. This happens just as often today as it did in Jesus' time.

This reminds me of what happens after many national tragedies such as September 11th or Hurricane Katrina. I remember all of these television fundraisers with dozens of celebrities. It was almost like a contest among the Hollywood elite to see who would could raise the most money. There were a few who even went onto talk shows and held press conferences announcing how much they donated. While it is great they were giving, it's probably safe to say that they got their reward.

Giving is a private matter

I'm not going to get into how much we should give or to whom; that is between God and ourselves. When we give, we should pray over it. Let God lead us to decide how much we should give and to whom. When we do give, we should pray that what we have given goes to help others and ultimately to advance God's Kingdom. When possible, we should not let others know. God knows what we gave and that is what's important. The person sitting next to us in church doesn't need to know, nor does our pastor even. I've seen people in church who will whip out a wad of bills and make a big show of counting them out, loudly crinkling them, so that all might see. This is the kind of showmanship that Jesus scorns.

Like many of the messages before this one, Jesus' focus is not on the external, but the internal. Jesus says that giving is fine, but it's how and why you give that is important. This recalls the theme that is repeated over and over in this sermon: discipleship is more than external actions.

Mt 6:5 *And when you pray, do not be like the hypocrites, for they love to pray standing in the synagogues and on the street corners to be seen by men. I tell you the truth, they have received their reward in full.*

Mt 6:6 *But when you pray, go into your room, close the door and pray to your Father, who is unseen. Then your Father, who sees what is done in secret, will reward you.*

Mt 6:7 *And when you pray, do not keep on babbling like pagans, for they think they will be heard because of their many words.*

Mt 6:8 *Do not be like them, for your Father knows what you need before you ask him.*

Mt 6:9 *"This, then, is how you should pray: " 'Our Father in heaven, hallowed be your name,*

Mt 6:10 *your kingdom come, your will be done on earth as it is in heaven.*

Mt 6:11 *Give us today our daily bread.*

Mt 6:12 *Forgive us our debts, as we also have forgiven our debtors.*

Mt 6:13 *And lead us not into temptation, but deliver us from the evil one.'*

Mt 6:14 *For if you forgive men when they sin against you, your heavenly Father will also forgive you.*

Mt 6:15 *But if you do not forgive men their sins, your Father will not forgive your sins.*

18.
Teach Us How to Pray

In this passage, Jesus gives us a model of how to pray. This prayer is often known as the "Lord's Prayer," although it should be called the "disciples prayer" since he was giving it to those of us who would be his disciples. Just as with the issue of giving to the poor, Jesus isn't as concerned with exact words as much as he is concerned with intentions. He cares about the heart of the person praying. Are we praying to help ourselves and to benefit ourselves, or are we pursuing God's will?

Do not pray like the hypocrites

Jesus comes out swinging in this passage. He criticizes those who thrive off of public prayer and who make a big production of their prayers. Now, there is nothing wrong with public prayer. I don't think Jesus is condemning that. The church we attend has a twenty-four hour house of prayer. During some of these times, they have an open microphone time when people can walk up and take turns praying for a few minutes at a time. This is a form of corporate prayer. However, we need to check ourselves and be sure our motives are pure when we pray in public. We must always ask ourselves whose glory we are seeking.

The hypocrites stand in public and make sure everyone around them sees and hears their prayers. Jesus uses the pagans who would repeat certain phrases over and over as an example.

They thought the gods would be more likely to hear them or to answer them if they used more words. Jesus says this is not the case. As with all biblical passages, it is easy to get too carried away with an extreme. I've known many who take that verse about repetition to a new level. They would say that it is a sin, perhaps even idolatrous, to repeat any phrase in a prayer or song more than once for any reason, at any time, ever. Some would even condemn certain worship songs just because of repeating choruses. I don't believe that is what Jesus was talking about. Here is why:

Isa 6:1 In the year that King Uzziah died, I saw the Lord seated on a throne, high and exalted, and the train of his robe filled the temple.
Isa 6:2 Above him were seraphs, each with six wings: With two wings they covered their faces, with two they covered their feet, and with two they were flying.
Isa 6:3 And they were calling to one another: "Holy, holy , holy is the LORD Almighty; the whole earth is full of his glory."

The angels sing, "Holy, holy, holy is the Lord Almighty," over and over in God's presence, and he doesn't tire of it. I can't imagine he'd regard our worship any differently. Jesus seems to be telling us that chanting, yelling, and babbling, much like what we see when Elijah challenges the prophets of Baal in 1 Kings 18, isn't necessary. There, the prophets yelled, pranced, chanted, cried, and even cut themselves to try to get their god's attention. The pagan culture at Jesus' time wasn't much different.

Pray in your closet

This doesn't mean we must always pray in a literal closet.

He's saying to pray privately. Even in public, it's possible to pray silently or privately. I will probably get myself into some trouble with this next line of thought. I've never been real big on praying before meals, especially in restaurants. I've caught a lot of flack from other Christians for this too.

I've heard comments like, "You're studying to be a pastor and you don't say grace before meals?" Well, I do say grace, but not always right then and there. One thing I find interesting is that you don't see a lot of examples of prayer before meals in the Bible. It does happen, of course. Jesus blessed the bread and fish before he fed the 5,000. I feel I have good reasons for not saying a public grace, and maybe my reticence to do so is something I need to get over, but let me tell you why I feel the way I do.

I grew up in a church with a lot of religionists. There were many people in this church who would pray in public places, and they often made a big show of it. They weren't super loud, but they were loud enough that people around them could hear. Some people would argue that this is a good witness and a good testimony, and they may be right. I'm not judging anyone who does this. However, for the people I saw doing it, it was a legalistic practice. You weren't a good Christian if you didn't do what they did. They were also quite proud of themselves. They were much like the Pharisee in Luke 18:10-14. So perhaps I've overcompensated because I don't want to be like them. I do, however, try to live a life of prayer and thanksgiving.

Forgive others, so that you might be forgiven.

This is the last thing Jesus tells us in this passage after reciting his prayer model. He mentions it in the prayer itself, but then he says it again after the prayer. This would mean it's an important point. Some might ask, "You mean I have to forgive others before God will forgive me?" I hate to answer a question with a question, but my response to that usually is, "Why should he?" Look at the price Jesus paid: pain, humiliation, and death. He was beaten, tortured, spit on, nailed to a piece of wood, and left to bake in the hot sun. He did all that so we might know him and join him in eternity. He paid our debt for us.

So if we respond to his truly heavenly gift by holding grudges against others, what does he owe us? He never owed us anything to begin with. Just take a look at his parable of the unmerciful servant in Matthew 18:23-35. No sin anyone ever commits against us can come close to what we have committed against God. Yet he forgave us. We should have been on that cross, but he took our place. Asking us to forgive those who have wronged us, whether they ask for our forgiveness or not, is a rather small request.

^{Mt 6:16} *When you fast, do not look somber as the hypocrites do, for they disfigure their faces to show men they are fasting. I tell you the truth, they have received their reward in full.*
^{Mt 6:17} *But when you fast, put oil on your head and wash your face,* ^{Mt 6:18} *so that it will not be obvious to men that you are fasting, but only to your Father, who is unseen; and your Father, who sees what is done in secret, will reward you.*

19.
When You Fast

This is probably one of the most overlooked passages in the Sermon on the Mount. Jesus gives us some guidelines on how to go about fasting. Fasting for some reason isn't practiced very often today. Honestly, when was the last time any of us can say we fasted? This is something even I struggle with. Though I have been working on it, this one can be one of the more challenging things Jesus presents us with.

Jesus didn't say "if"

One of the things in this passage that jumps out is that Jesus did not say, "if you fast." He instead says, "when you fast." Some people take this as a command ordering us to fast. I don't know if we could go that far with this or with any other part of the Sermon on the Mount. Throughout this entire sermon, Jesus is not so much telling us what to do as he is telling us how to do it. However, he doesn't give fasting any less emphasis than he does prayer. So perhaps we are missing out on something by not fasting.

Don't be like the hypocrites

There is that word again, "hypocrites." Jesus tells us not to make a show of our spirituality. This is one of the running themes throughout this sermon. Fasting, just like prayer or any other spiritual discipline, should be between God and ourselves. Just as in Jesus' time, many today enjoy making a show of their godliness. During Jesus' time, some would purposely look sick or weak and make sure that everyone around them knew they were fasting. This was not acceptable to Jesus back then, nor is it now. Once again, it's not what we're doing, but how we do it and where our heart is in the process.

Fasting is between God and ourselves

Only God should know we are fasting. When we boast to others about fasting, prayer, giving, or whatever, we are glorifying ourselves and not God. Sure, we may get a few pats on the back and some "Amens," but, as Jesus said, we have received our reward. Now, as I've mentioned earlier, that doesn't mean it's wrong for anyone to know what we are doing or for us to tell anyone. I suppose if co-workers insist that you eat lunch with them and they keep asking you why you're not eating, there is probably a subtle way to let someone know why you aren't eating. Whatever the situation, we just need to evaluate our motives.

We should evaluate our motives for fasting it in the first place. Are we fasting to grow spiritually? Are we doing it to be closer to God? Might we be doing it to look holy before men? With Jesus, motive is everything. So often, we get so caught up in the details of what we are doing: should we fast for 12 hours or 24 hours, should we drink juice, should we drink anything, eat fruit, etc. I just don't get the feeling that Jesus is as worried about the details of our actions as he is about the spirit behind them. As I said earlier, obedience is more than external acts.

Before we begin a fast, we should pray and ask God to lead us as to how we are to go about it. We should ask him to make our hearts and motives pure. While we are fasting, we should devote more time to God. As we fast, we are purifying our bodies from all the externals of this world and feasting instead on God. We are handing our flesh over to him and relying on him. Just as the ancient Israelites in the desert collecting manna, we too are relying on God for nourishment.

Mt 6:19 *Do not store up for yourselves treasures on earth, where moth and rust destroy, and where thieves break in and steal.*
Mt 6:20 *But store up for yourselves treasures in heaven, where moth and rust do not destroy, and where thieves do not break in and steal.*
Mt 6:21 *For where your treasure is, there your heart will be also.*
Mt 6:22 *The eye is the lamp of the body. If your eyes are good, your whole body will be full of light.*
Mt 6:23 *But if your eyes are bad, your whole body will be full of darkness. If then the light within you is darkness, how great is that darkness!*
Mt 6:24 *No one can serve two masters. Either he will hate the one and love the other, or he will be devoted to the one and despise the other. You cannot serve both God and Money.*

20.
Digging for Treasure

Have any of you watched pirate movies? I remember reading *Treasure Island* when I was a kid. That was a fun story We used to play pirates as kids as well. We would even get a fake eye-patch and run around with sticks for swords. We would wave the sticks around and swashbuckle around our back yard looking for buried treasure. Arrrrr! Okay, so I'm getting carried away. Seriously, though, I remember digging up our yard and my grandma's garden during one summer when I was a kid. My friends and I were seriously looking for treasure. Granted, we were about ten years old. The only thing we ever found were rocks and some old cow bones.

When we grow up, our search for treasure doesn't stop. We get jobs and careers, and we often try to move up the ladder. We'll do anything to make another dollar so we can buy that new toy. We think that if only our house were just a little bigger or our car a little newer, our lives would be better. In this passage, Jesus tells us just what all of these things are good for, and which treasures we should be digging for.

Treasures of this world are temporary

We spend our whole lives working to build up earthly wealth. Several years ago, I worked as a nurse's aide in a nursing home. I enjoyed taking care of the elderly. However, I noticed something quite interesting. There were many residents there who had lived long, successful lives. They had built lifetimes of financial security and had nice houses, cars, and money. No sooner were many of them finally able to retire and enjoy their wealth, then they had a stroke, a heart attack, or a serious fall. Before they knew what had happened, they were in the nursing home. All of that money and wealth would be gone in less than a year in order to pay for their health care. So there they were, near the end of their lives, going out with the exact same thing with which they came into this world: nothing.

Don't get me wrong. It is not my intention to condemn the wealthy. I don't believe Jesus was saying having money or wealth is a sin. Problems occur when we put our faith and security in our wealth. All sorts of things can happen: wars, natural disasters, health crises. All of these things can wipe out a lifetime of wealth and riches without a moment's notice. Without permanent riches to rest on, we will be in big trouble.

Treasure in heaven is permanent

Years ago I read about a local preacher who loaded his congregation onto a bus and took them to a junkyard for their church service. As they arrived, they filed off the bus, not sure what to think. He walked them through the junkyard and showed them all of the broken and rusted cars, burned out TVs, and busted stereo systems. He wanted to show them where all of their material possessions would one day end up.

I worked a part-time job several years ago at a funeral home. I did a variety of tasks around the home, so that the funeral directors could focus on preparing the bodies and making funeral arrangements. One of my duties was driving the hearse at funerals. I drove hearses for many funerals, and never once was there a U-Haul attached to take the deceased's earthly possessions with them.

God's treasures, however, are permanent.

1Pe 5:4 And when the Chief Shepherd appears, you will receive the crown of glory that will never fade away.

No one can serve two masters

Jesus doesn't beat around the bush on this one. We either serve God, or we serve money. This is evidenced by the story of the rich young ruler in Matthew 19:16. That young man, when given the choice to follow God or keep his wealth, chose his wealth. I have seen many Christians make that fateful choice. Sure, they want to go to church and maybe even teach Sunday school or get involved in some other ministry, but what is closest to their hearts is their money.

As I've said, money is not evil, nor is having money wrong. I know many godly people who have been blessed financially and have used that blessing to further God's kingdom. Unfortunately, many others have dedicated their lives to chasing the dollar at all costs. If we do have money, we can either control it or let it control us. We need to ask ourselves, "Which master do we serve?" This is why we must choose just where we will dig for treasure.

Mt 6:25 *Therefore I tell you, do not worry about your life,*
what you will eat or drink; or about your body,
what you will wear. Is not life more important than food,
and the body more important than clothes?
Mt 6:26 *Look at the birds of the air; they do not sow or reap or store*
away in barns, and yet your heavenly Father feeds them.
Are you not much more valuable than they?
Mt 6:27 *Who of you by worrying can add a single hour to his life?*
Mt 6:28 *And why do you worry about clothes? See how the lilies of the*
field grow. They do not labor or spin.
Mt 6:29 *Yet I tell you that not even Solomon in all his splendor was*
dressed like one of these.
Mt 6:30 *If that is how God clothes the grass of the field,*
which is here today and tomorrow is thrown into the fire,
will he not much more clothe you, O you of little faith?
Mt 6:31 *So do not worry, saying,*
'What shall we eat?' or 'What shall we drink?
or 'What shall we wear?'
Mt 6:32 *For the pagans run after all these things,*
and your heavenly Father knows that you need them.
Mt 6:33 *But seek first his kingdom and his righteousness,*
and all these things will be given to you as well.
Mt 6:34 *Therefore do not worry about tomorrow, for tomorrow will*
worry about itself. Each day has enough trouble of its own.

21.
Don't Worry

How many people today are filled with worry and anxiety? We live in a society that is fast paced, tough, and even brutal at times. Most of us have rent or mortgages, car payments, credit cards, and other debts. It can be hard to keep up with all of this while trying to make sure all of our needs our met. Many Americans suffer from anxiety disorder. I myself even deal with mild cases of anxiety. Why do we do this? What makes us put ourselves through this? If we truly follow Jesus, do we need to worry about these things? Jesus tells us in Matthew 6:25-34 precisely how we should approach worry.

Do not worry about your life

Jesus starts off by listing those things we need not worry about. He includes food, drink, and clothing. These are the essentials of life. Yet Jesus tells us not to worry about these things. Keep in mind that when Jesus spoke these words, items such as food, clothing, and water were not a given in society. People had to hunt and grow their food and either had to dig wells for their water or walk long distances to the nearest wells. Only the rich had nice clothing, while the poor had basic robes and rags. It was against this social backdrop that Jesus told his disciples not to worry. If people shouldn't have worried back then, why should we worry today when such necessities are plentiful?

Birds of the air do not worry

Jesus used birds as an example. Each day, birds go out and find just the food they need for that day. They live day to day Every day, God sees to it that they have what they need. Jesus tells us here we are worth more than the birds. If God will provide for them, then he will provide for us. It might not be the richest, nicest, or most lavish things, but we will have what we need.

Worry will not add one single hour to your life

Jesus uses grass as an example in this section. I know you may be thinking, "Grass doesn't wear clothes." Yet God provides them with their color, their shape, and their food. Jesus also uses lilies as another example. They are beautiful flowers. King Solomon, the richest king in the world, who had the finest clothes in the land, wasn't even adorned as well as a lily. That is because lilies are each dressed by God. God takes the time to make sure the grass has its color and body. Even though it will be walked on, eaten by cattle, or even burned, God takes care of it. If he takes time to care for these little things, won't he take care of us?

I purposely left out the last part of verse 30: "Oh you of little faith." When we worry, isn't faith what we are lacking? As I said, not worrying is often a struggle for me as I suffer from mild anxiety. My problem is usually situational. If I have something stressful going on with work or family, I tend to obsess over it. Then I'll keep thinking about it and repeatedly play little mind games with myself over what is going to happen. Then I'll wonder if I should do something about it.

I'm doing much better with this. Years ago I regularly made a mess of things. Now I'm doing better at learning patience and learning to let things go. I'm growing in faith. After all, didn't God provide food for the people of Israel for 40 years in the desert? If so, I would imagine he could help us make it through until our next paycheck. We make things too hard on ourselves. As Jesus tells us, tomorrow will worry about itself. Each day has its own troubles. We can always fall back on Jesus' two most comforting words: Don't worry.

Mt 7:1 Do not judge, or you too will be judged.

Mt 7:2 For in the same way you judge others, you will be judged, and with the measure you use, it will be measured to you.

Mt 7:3 Why do you look at the speck of sawdust in your brother's eye and pay no attention to the plank in your own eye?

Mt 7:4 How can you say to your brother, 'Let me take the speck out of your eye,' when all the time there is a plank in your own eye?

Mt 7:5 You hypocrite, first take the plank out of your own eye, and then you will see clearly to remove the speck from your brother's eye.

Mt 7:6 Do not give dogs what is sacred; do not throw your pearls to pigs. If you do, they may trample them under their feet, and then turn and tear you to pieces.

22.
Judge Not

J udge not!" That's what the Bible says, and that's what we often hear from both the Christian and secular world. Anytime anyone is critical of anything, the "judge not" passage comes flying. So what does this really mean? What is judgment? Does this mean we must silently watch everyone around us do things we know are wrong? Some would have us believe so. In my own experience, I've seen this passage abused many times over. People are quick to throw this in someone's face when they are called out for doing even the worst things. As a result, many of us are afraid to use any form of judgment or discernment.

Do not judge others

Judgment is not something to be taken lightly. When we go around pointing fingers, we not only expose the person whom we are judging, but we also expose ourselves. We are inviting others to hold us to the same standard with which we are judging, but we also expose ourselves. For example, if I were cheating on my wife, and I fond out someone else in church was cheating on his, then I probably would not the best person to be confronting this other person. My own standard of judgment can be used against me.

Mind the plank in your own eye

If any of us has a problem with pornography, alcohol, or any other addiction, we're probably not the best one to point out another's sin for watching some trivial television program. I've been to churches were people were quick to slam a parent for allowing their kids to attend prom, but, in the long run, those very people who were making those condemnations were doing things that were much worse. If our own house isn't in order, how can we clean someone else's? Jesus goes on to say that when we do this, we make ourselves hypocrites. We talked earlier about what Jesus thought of hypocrites. The "hypocrite" column is not a good category in which to be.

Remove the plank from your own eye

Once we have gotten our house in order, then we can help another. If a man in the church goes into recovery for his alcoholism, and he gets and stays clean for a period of time, then he can approach a brother who is going downhill with his drinking and say, "Hey, brother, you're out of bounds. You need help." However, we need to make sure that what we are doing is done out of love. Righteous judgment is always done in love and with the intention of restoring the offender.

I knew a woman a few years ago who was cheating on her husband with a man from her church. Both of them thought they were clever and were fooling everyone. They went to church every Sunday with their families as if nothing were wrong. The truth was, everyone in the church knew. Finally, the pastor and some deacons pulled her aside and politely told her, "Sister, we love you, but this has got to stop." They talked to her at some length and ended up counseling her as she broke down. She told me this shook her to her core. She knew what she had been doing was wrong and that she couldn't hide it from God. Once her sin was exposed, she repented and got right with God and her family. Without loving and godly judgment, she would have continued in her sin until both families were destroyed.

So it would seem that, in this passage, Jesus is not telling us to never use any form of judgment at all. Something to keep in mind is that the religious leaders of this time seriously oppressed the Jewish people. They were quick to condemn anyone who did not follow their rules and traditions to the letter. Jesus here is telling us to judge righteously. We are not judging the person, but their actions. As with all things, judgment it is to be made with love, compassion, and with the goal of restoring the sinner to God.

Mt 7:7 *Ask and it will be given to you; seek and you will find; knock and the door will be opened to you.*

Mt 7:8 *For everyone who asks receives; he who seeks finds; and to him who knocks, the door will be opened.*

Mt 7:9 *Which of you, if his son asks for bread, will give him a stone?*

Mt 7:10 *Or if he asks for a fish, will give him a snake?*

Mt 7:11 *If you, then, though you are evil, know how to give good gifts to your children, how much more will your Father in heaven give good gifts to those who ask him!*

Mt 7:12 *So in everything, do to others what you would have them do to you, for this sums up the Law and the Prophets.*

23

Ask, Seek, Knock

J esus goes on to describe how we may go about finding him. By this time in the Sermon on the Mount, he has already talked about how we can empty ourselves and live for him. He has given us instructions on how to live and has detailed what kind of attitudes we should have. In this passage, he sort of repeats part of the Beatitudes. He told us before how to seek after him in order to be blessed. Here, he reminds us again that finding him is not as difficult as we often make it out to be.

Everyone who asks, receives

This part of the passage is often misquoted. Jesus is not saying that we will get anything and everything that we ask of him. Anyone who thinks that needs to go back and read the rest of the sermon. He says, "Ask, and it will be given to you." What will be given? Since he talks so much throughout his message about the Kingdom of God, it would make sense to assume that is what will be given to you.

We focus so much on the idea of eternal life, which Jesus does talk about, so this assumption is correct. However, he's not limiting this statement to the afterlife. If Jesus were simply talking about having eternal life, he wouldn't have given this big sermon on how to live for God. We can live in his Kingdom here on earth by following the simple yet tough instructions he left for us.

Everyone who seeks, finds

Jesus will not hide himself from those who seek him. I can't think of a single person who sought after Jesus with a sincere heart who didn't find him. Just as Jesus says in verse nine, God is your father. Just as none of us would give our hungry children a stone, God will not deny his children who hunger for him. Remember how Jesus blessed those who hunger and thirst for righteousness? Their blessing is the nourishment of God, his Kingdom.

For everyone who knocks, the door will be opened

God's Kingdom is not a night club with some list of admissible names. You don't have to be a member or pay dues to be "in." It's not a country club or even a book club. God is not impressed with elite or exclusive man-made memberships. As Christians today, we have erected many of our own barriers. We decide who gets in. Only people who look, think, and act like us can take part. That is quite sad, because God has not done this to a single one of us. If God had created an exclusive club, not a single one of us would be worthy to join. He accepts us as we are, where we are. The only thing we need to do is knock.

Jesus ends his message in verse twelve with what we know as the Golden Rule. This, he says, sums up the law and the prophets. Everything he has talked about so far has dealt with how we treat others. Even in this passage, where he is telling us how to find him, he concludes with the same theme: taking care of others. I have worked on this book for a year, and the more I dig into these passages, the easier they are to understand.

We have made this section of the Bible so difficult, but what Jesus is saying isn't that hard at all. We've dissected his words, legalized them, and dismissed them to the point that most of us don't even bother with them anymore. The Sermon on the Mount was never meant to be a legalistic set of rules as some would have it. Legalism is exactly the opposite of what Jesus is promoting throughout his sermon. I've gained so much more understanding of his words by simply praying before reading them and by just taking to heart what he is actually saying and his reasons for saying it. As we approach the last few chapters of this book, I hope that every reader now better understands what Jesus was telling us.

Mt 7:13 *Enter through the narrow gate. For wide is the gate and broad is the road that leads to destruction, and many enter through it.* *Mt 7:14* *But small is the gate and narrow the road that leads to life, and only a few find it.*

24.

The Wide Gate to Destruction

I'm sure most of us have seen some TV preachers holding large revivals or crusades. They tell us all we have to do is say this prayer, send so much money, or do some other magical thing in order to enter God's Kingdom. We wish it were that easy, don't we? How about Oprah Winfrey? She talks about God, but she seems to focus on some kind of pop spirituality devoid of repentance and transformation. She focuses on earthly success and achievements. She and many others like to teach that there are many ways to God. These teachers preach about a wide gate into heaven.

Jesus, on the other hand, says something completely different. He teaches the opposite of this popular message. Keep in mind that he is not saying that God is selective or picky about who he chooses. As Jesus said in the previous passage, to anyone who knocks, the door will be opened. It is not God who is selective in choosing us. It is man who has become selective by not choosing God.

Enter through the narrow gate

What exactly is the narrow gate? I think the answer is pretty simple. Jesus has already been explaining the narrow gate throughout this sermon. He has not just been giving us instructions on how to live; he has also been telling us what the nature of our hearts should be. He doesn't just tell us what to do; he tells us who we should become.

So many of us today practice "Cafeteria Christianity." We go through the line and pick and choose what we will believe and how we will follow God. We insist on following God on our own terms. I've had countless people ask me how to be closer to God. I tell them to seek his face. I suggest things like daily prayer, quiet time, studying the Bible, and finding key passages to meditate on and pray over. I will even suggest they find a group of fellow believers (not necessarily a church) with which to fellowship.

In many of those cases, I get a response like, "I don't have time for all that. Why doesn't God just move closer to us?" Well, the answer to that is simple. He is the almighty creator of the universe. If we won't make time for him, why should he make time for us? As busy as we may think we are, I'm sure God has plenty more to do, yet he always makes time to be with us if we call out to him.

You may also encounter what many call "easy believism" or "cheap grace." You say the "sinner's prayer," and then, as if you've completed a business transaction, you're saved. All you have to do is say this specific prayer (which just so happens to be nowhere in the Bible) and poof! You're saved. From that point on, you just kick back and cruise into heaven. In many cases in which the "sinner's prayer" is prayed, there has been no change or transformation at all.

As I discussed earlier, the Kingdom isn't just going to heaven after we die. It's the life Jesus showed us we can live here and now. I'm going to be careful here. I'm not saying we must live this way to make it into heaven or that we must work or earn our way to heaven. I'm not saying anything like that. I'm saying that committing your life to Jesus is much more than a one time act of faith.

The path Jesus outlines for us in this sermon is not an easy path. It can be downright hard and even impossible to live by. He shows us how difficult it is in order to show us how much we need him. We cannot do any of this with our own strength. We won't even come close to reaching God's ideal. He never tells us to become converts or to just say a prayer and then wait to die. He calls us to be disciples, to take up our crosses and follow him.

Mt 16:24 *Then Jesus said to his disciples, "If anyone would come after me, he must deny himself and take up his cross and follow me.*

The wide gate leads to destruction

This is the gate that so many will go through. Why would people choose this one? Because it is wider and easier to go through. So we say a sinner's prayer, donate some money, and sit in church twice a week without experiencing true repentance, life change, or transformation of any kind within our hearts. That is the wide gate. None of these things is necessarily bad, but nor are they the means of our salvation.

When a TV personality tells us to mix various religions together to suit our own purposes, that is the wide gate. Doing whatever we want in life as if there is no God in heaven is the wide gate. The wide gate will lead to destruction.

For many years, I did my own thing. We live in a country where we don't like to be told what to do. Not only do we like doing our own thing, but it is almost considered wrong to tell someone he is out of bounds. We all want to have our own truth. Yet there can only be one truth. I thought I had my own truth years ago, but my truth almost destroyed my life.

I've talked to some who have said they are seeking the narrow gate, but not right now. The wide gate is more convenient for the moment. While I feel sad for those people, that is their choice to make. God isn't going to twist anyone's arm, and it is not my intention to scare anyone. However, Jesus has laid the groundwork for us to find him. All we need to do is knock.

The narrow gate leads to life

Jn 14:6 Jesus answered, "I am the way and the truth and the life. No one comes to the Father except through me.

If the narrow gate leads to life, why do so few find it? As we saw earlier, the wide gate is much easier, much more palatable. Isn't the harder way more worthwhile? I know I've found in life that the things that offer the greatest reward are the things for which I have to work the hardest. When you talk to any athlete who has won a championship, he will tell you how hard it was and how much work it required. Sure, he could have just done the bare minimum and made some money through his career; or he could work twice as hard for twice as long and get the big prize.

When in school, Michael Jordan would practice and workout for hours and hours a day while his friends were out having fun. Likewise, Peyton Manning would watch game films and study opponents while his classmates were out partying. Both of these men could have taken the easy route and had fun while living for the moment, but they would not have reaped the rewards that their hard work produced. We must do the same thing. The Apostle Paul tells us:

1Co 9:25 Everyone who competes in the games goes into strict training. They do it to get a crown that will not last; but we do it to get a crown that will last forever.

1Co 9:26 Therefore I do not run like a man running aimlessly; I do not fight like a man beating the air.
1Co 9:27 No, I beat my body and make it my slave so that after I have preached to others, I myself will not be disqualified for the prize.

Living for God is like training for the Super Bowl or for a marathon. We must work and train and teach ourselves to be more like Jesus. This is the narrow gate. The wide gate promises temporary fun and instant gratification. The narrow gate promises hard work, humility, and a life of servant living, but the end result is a much bigger and everlasting prize. Even if we fail constantly, I had a pastor once tell me, "It's better to fail at a cause that will ultimately succeed than to succeed at a cause that will ultimately fail." Our success is guaranteed through the narrow gate.

Mt 7:15 *Watch out for false prophets. They come to you in sheep's clothing, but inwardly they are ferocious wolves.*

Mt 7:16 *By their fruit you will recognize them. Do people pick grapes from thornbushes, or figs from thistles?*

Mt 7:17 *Likewise every good tree bears good fruit, but a bad tree bears bad fruit.*

Mt 7:18 *A good tree cannot bear bad fruit, and a bad tree cannot bear good fruit.*

Mt 7:19 *Every tree that does not bear good fruit is cut down and thrown into the fire.*

Mt 7:20 *Thus, by their fruit you will recognize them.*

Mt 7:21 *"Not everyone who says to me, 'Lord, Lord,' will enter the kingdom of heaven, but only he who does the will of my Father who is in heaven.*

Mt 7:22 *Many will say to me on that day, 'Lord, Lord, did we not prophesy in your name, and in your name drive out demons and perform many miracles?'*

Mt 7:23 *Then I will tell them plainly, 'I never knew you. Away from me, you evildoers!'*

25.

You Will Know Them By Their Fruit

In Matthew 7:15-23, Jesus warns us against false prophets and false teachers. I'm sure most of us have known a false prophet; we may not even have realized it at the time. They, probably dressed nicely, come in among us. They may say all of the things we want to hear, and they might even have a miracle or two up their sleeves. The problem is, the things they teach are wrong. They teach a different Jesus. Instead of teaching the Jesus of the Bible, they teach their own, made-up version of Jesus.

One of the most popular teachings infecting churches today is this vision of Jesus that is based on the American dream. Some have superimposed teachings of money and power onto Jesus and his life. They have made him this Americanized combination of Bob Dylan and Donald Trump: some laid back guy with a bunch of cool sayings who wants us all to be rich. As we have seen throughout this sermon, Jesus taught the exact opposite.

False prophets come in sheep's clothing

Most false teachers don't show up with a sign on their forehead that says, "WARNING: False Prophet." They are usually handsome, well dressed, and eloquent speakers. They may even be photogenic with a million dollar smile and perfect hair. On the surface, they seem perfect and flawless. What could be wrong with such people?

Even when they talk, most of what they say might be true. I've heard some say, "What's the big deal if they are only one degree off?" Well, what happens to an aircraft trying to land on an aircraft carrier if it's just one degree off? The plane will end up at the bottom of the ocean. I've heard it said that the best lies are 90% truth. That is why we must take everything we hear from any preacher and compare it with scripture. If anything a person says doesn't line up, then it's time to start asking questions.

I want to clarify here that I'm not talking about minor differences in interpretation. I've been in many healthy debates over eternal security and free will and other various doctrines and theories. What I am talking about are things that are clearly false or taken completely out of context. Sometimes I have heard things that are just completely made up. One good example to follow when listening to any teacher is that of the Bereans:

Ac 17:11 Now the Bereans were of more noble character than the Thessalonians, for they received the message with great eagerness and examined the Scriptures every day to see if what Paul said was true.

You will know them by their fruit

As Jesus says, a good tree will bear good fruit. He is saying this is true of any teacher. A good teacher will produce good fruit. His church will be filled with loving and growing disciples. It might not be a large church, but it will bear good fruit. Let's compare this to what happens with a false teacher.

Think back to any church you have attended that had a false teacher. I can think of at least one I've attended in the past. From my own experience, the people in such churches range from cold and self-righteous to shallow and superficial. I suppose I'm making some generalizations here, but, as I said, this is based on my own experience. Think back to your own experiences with such churches or teachers and see what you find. I've often heard it said that a church takes on the personality of its pastor. So if you attend a cold or superficial church, there is one place to look for the reason why the people act as they do.

Not everyone who says, "Lord, Lord" will enter the Kingdom

Verse 22 is another one that often gets twisted around. Many people live in fear that they will be cast away from Jesus, as if he has some sort of random selection process. That is not the case at all. What he is saying is that more is required than simply acknowledging he is Lord. Even demons know who Jesus is (Mk 5:1-20). Jesus is also saying that just doing some good deeds isn't good enough. He's been saying that throughout this entire message. He's just repeating that fact here.

If you look at the overall context of this passage, you will see that Jesus is talking about false prophets. They declare the name of Jesus and toss his name around as if it's some magical formula. They might even have a "WWJD" bumper sticker or bracelet. As the passage says, they might prophesy in Jesus' name. Maybe they teach Sunday school or lead a Bible study. They might even pastor a church, but, deep down, they don't really know Jesus.

This failure to get to know Jesus truly is something that could happen to any of us. We might know religion and all the right things, but we might not really know God. It's one thing to know about him; it's another thing to truly know him. This is what Jesus is talking about in this passage and throughout his whole sermon. Knowing Christ is much more than giving intellectual assent to some concepts or subscribing to a specific set of ideas. Knowing Christ is about letting him penetrate every fiber of your being. This starts with obedience, but not just outward obedience: it starts with an obedient heart.

Mt 7:24 *Therefore everyone who hears these words of mine and puts them into practice is like a wise man who built his house on the rock.* Mt 7:25 *The rain came down, the streams rose, and the winds blew and beat against that house; yet it did not fall, because it had its foundation on the rock.* Mt 7:26 *But everyone who hears these words of mine and does not put them into practice is like a foolish man who built his house on sand.* Mt 7:27 *The rain came down, the streams rose, and the winds blew and beat against that house, and it fell with a great crash.*

26.
What Kind of a Builder Are You?

Here we come to the final passage of Jesus' sermon. He picks an excellent way of concluding his message. Jesus tells us that we shouldn't just listen to his words, but that we should apply them to our lives. How many of us sit in church on Sunday, sing all the songs, listen to the message (and even take notes), and then forget everything we heard the instant we step outside of the walls? Jesus is warning us against this.

Jesus' words are like a rock

The wise man here built his house on the rock. I remember singing that song in Sunday school. Jesus' words are like the rock. If we live by the things he has taught us, we cannot fail. We might seem to fail by earthly standards, but we will have succeeded by heavenly standards. The words of Jesus are firm; if we stand on them and live by them, we cannot be shaken.

Not putting his words into practice is foolish

I'm not sure why we fail to put God's words into practice. I find myself disregarding God's word sometimes. In the past year, I've been doing better. It so often seems like we will read and study the Bible but then go on about our business as if nothing has changed. God's Word causes change! It is living and breathing. The words of Jesus are life giving and life changing. I don't know how I could just passively read the Bible for so long and not be changed each and every time I read it.

If we do read or hear his words, and we are not affected in some way, then it is time we make a close examination of ourselves. Jesus scolds the Pharisees several times for knowing the scriptures and knowing the words but not knowing him. We can know him through his words. If we know the most holy God, his words will have an impact on us. Jesus tells us that those of us who do not put his words into practice are like foolish men.

Foolishness leads to destruction

We see what happens to the foolish man in this passage: his house is destroyed. A similar fate awaits those who choose the wide gate that I discussed earlier. Despite all the warnings and words of wisdom, the foolish will build upon the sand. When I was in the Marines, I was stationed in California. I remember seeing these huge mansions built along hillsides. Do you know what was supporting these things? Stilts. That's right, about three or four long, wooden stilts or beams were going up from the hillside to the home to support it. Every year in the winter months, it rained heavily. Every year these homes would slide down the hills, and every year people were surprised at what happened. It just blew me away. Those houses made me think of this passage.

We may build on our personal wealth, or our vast education, degrees, and knowledge. We might even build on our power, titles, and positions. All of these things will not withstand the heavy storms of life. Every one of them is sinking sand. I remember singing this hymn when I was a kid:

On Christ the solid rock I stand,
all other ground is sinking sand,
all other ground is sinking sand.

This passage concludes Jesus' own words. I find it interesting how he started out calmly and with uplifting words before he gradually began pushing and pushing our buttons to make his points. This passage provides a good summary of everything he said in the Sermon on the Mount. Yet what have we as Christians actually done with his words? As this book draws to a close, I pray that everyone reading this has gained some insight into Jesus' words and a better understanding of his message.

Mt 7:28 *When Jesus had finished saying these things,*
the crowds were amazed at his teaching,
Mt 7:29 *because he taught as one who had authority,*
and not as their teachers of the law.

CONCLUSION

The final two verses in these chapters are not Jesus' words, but they hold a lot of power. For centuries, people have picked apart this sermon. It's been dissected so much that most Christians don't even try to understand it anymore. I've had many tell me that we could never live by Christ's teachings in the sermon, so what would be the point of studying it further? The point is that Jesus gave us these words for a reason.

I love that last verse, where it says, "He taught as one who had authority." He wasn't someone giving us his take on things (as I'm doing now). Jesus was telling us how it really is, and how it was always supposed to be. Just imagine what the world would be like if the Church today actually lived as Jesus says we should. The world would be completely upside down.

Instead, the few churches I have seen that strive to live out this message are condemned by other Christians. They are called cults, extremists, and even new age. I have some news for anyone who would accuse their brothers and sisters of such things. Jesus *was* an extremist. He was an extremist for the Father. He did anything to further the Kingdom, including giving his own life. If he did this for us, then we should be extremists for him. I don't mean that we should blow people up or resort to any form of violence or coercion. We can be extremists by living out his Kingdom in the way that he told us to: by loving others, turning the other cheek, and hungering for righteousness.

This book has been a year-long labor of love. God has touched my life in many ways as I've gone through this message. I've learned so much about him and how much he loves us. As you read this, I pray that he does the same for you. I pray that you are blessed and may gain a better understanding of Jesus' words so that you too may live for the Kingdom and live to the extreme for Christ.

3093502

Made in the USA